real life

pre-intermediate

WORKBOOK

contents

1 your life

* easy to do
** a bit harder
*** extra challenge

Vocabulary

Time twins

1 Match 1–6 and a–f to form sentences.

1 Henry is studying
2 My brother and I often look
3 I need to find
4 My sister is a nurse,
5 I wonder
6 Paula works in a nursery

a because she loves children.
b out when Picasso was born for my art project.
c she works in a hospital.
d after our little sister.
e for his exams.
f what my friends are doing now.

2 Complete the text with the words below.

[private doing do crazy divorced
twins ✓ similar interests personalities]

Hi, I'm Katy! I'm seventeen years old and I've got one brother – he's seventeen too. We're ¹*twins*. We're both tall with blond hair, so physically we're ²_____. Our ³_____ are very different – I like music and art and my brother, Alex, is ⁴_____ about sport! Our ⁵_____ are very different too – Alex is very sociable, but I'm quiet. We live with our mother because our parents are ⁶_____. This year I'm ⁷_____ my A-levels at school. We go to a ⁸_____ school and we work very hard. After school I want to ⁹_____ a course at university.

Grammar

Present simple

3 ***** Put the verbs in brackets into the correct form of the present simple.

1 Mark *loves* (love) football but he _____ (not play) every day.
2 We _____ (use) English when we _____ (write) emails.
3 I _____ (not have) any brothers or sisters, but my friend _____ (have) two sisters.
4 Sam _____ (not go out) very often, but I _____ (go out) every weekend.
5 David usually _____ (watch) sports on Saturdays but I _____ (watch) sports every day.
6 Maria and Mark sometimes _____ (arrive) at school late because they _____ (live) far away.

4 ***** Use the verbs in brackets to complete the sentences. There are some short answers.

1 A: Where *do* you *live*? (live)
  B: I _____ in Canada.
2 A: When ___ Pat ___ to school? (go)
  B: She ___ at 8 a.m.
3 A: ___ Greta and Tim ___ coffee? (like)
  B: Yes, they ___ .
4 A: ___ Marek ___ in a shop? (work)
  B: No, he ___ .
5 A: What time ___ Fay ___ home? (get)
  B: She ___ home at 11p.m.

Grammar Plus: Present simple: word order with time expressions

5 ****** Put the words in the correct order to make sentences.

1 goes out/Sheena/always/Saturdays/on
  Sheena always goes out on Saturdays.
2 don't/we/always/at home/have dinner
  _____ .
3 play the guitar/Francis/does/often
  _____ ?
4 I/have lunch/never/at school
  _____ .
5 go running/every day/they/do
  _____ ?
6 don't/usually/we/drink tea/in the morning
  _____ .

Present continuous

6 ⊛ Look at the picture. Use the verbs in brackets to complete the sentences about what the teenagers are doing.

1 Tom and Frank _are buying_ (buy) cinema tickets.
2 Lisa _____ (look) at shoes.
3 Rachel _____ (eat) a salad.
4 Louise and Jane _____ (not/eat) salad. They _____ (drink) coffee.
5 Brian _____ (wait) for a friend.
6 George _____ (go) to the gym.

7 ⊛⊛ Complete the questions and then answer them, using the picture in exercise 6.

1 _Are_ Tom and Frank _eating salad_? (eat salad)
  No, they're not.
2 What ___ Tom and Frank _____? (do)
  _____
3 ⌐ Rachel _____? (look at shoes)
  _____
4 Who _____? (look in a shop window)
  _____
5 ___ Brian _____? (go to the cinema)
  _____
6 Where ___ George _____ ? (go)
  _____
7 ___ Louise and Jane _____ ? (eat pizza)
  _____
8 What ___ Louise and Jane _____ ? (do)
  _____

Grammar reference

Present simple

Form

+	I/We/You/They	live	in Glasgow.
	He/She/It	lives	
−	I/We/You/They	do not (don't) live	
	He/She/It	does not (doesn't) live	
?	Do	I/we/you/they live	in Glasgow?
	Does	he/she/it	

Short answers	Yes, I/we/you/they **do**. No, I/we/you/they **do not (don't)**. Yes, he/she/it **does**. No, he/she/it **does not (doesn't)**.

Wh- questions

Where do I/we/you/they live?
When does he/she/it eat?

Time expressions

sometimes, often, usually, never, every day/week/morning, a lot, always

Word order with time expressions

Time expressions can go at the beginning or end of sentences. However, in present simple sentences the time expression usually goes before the <u>main verb</u> in a sentence:
*I **usually** <u>go</u> swimming on Sundays*
*We don't **usually** <u>have</u> breakfast together.*
*Does she **usually** <u>catch</u> the bus home?*

Present continuous

Form

+	I	am ('m) waiting	for Tom.
	He/She/It	is ('s) waiting	
	We/You/They	are ('re) waiting	
−	I	am not ('m not) waiting	
	He/She/It	is not ('s not) waiting	
	We/You/They	are not ('re not) waiting	
?	Am I		waiting for Tom?
	Is he/she/it		
	Are we/you/they		

Short answers	Yes, I **am**. / No, I **am ('m) not**. Yes, he/she/it **is**. / No, he/she/it **is not (isn't)**. Yes, we/you/they **are**. / No, we/you/they **are not (aren't)**.

Time expressions

at the moment, now, today, this week/summer/morning/ evening/afternoon

1

Vocabulary

Social life

1 Match a verb from column A with a noun from column B to make collocations.

A	B
1 go to	a shopping
2 go	b the beach
3 play	c a party
4 meet	d new people
5 make	e computer games
6 have	f sport
7 do	g plans

2 Complete the paragraph with the verbs below.

> go x3   play   go to x2   do x2   stay
> meet ✓   make   have

About ME

I have a very busy social life! I ¹ _meet_ my friends nearly every day. We spend a lot of time together! At the weekend, we usually ² _____ the cinema. We all love films! After the film, we ³ _____ shopping and ⁴ _____ plans for the evening. Sometimes, we ⁵ _____ a party or just ⁶ _____ video games. I often ⁷ _____ sport or ⁸ _____ running in the holidays. I ⁹ _____ the swimming pool a lot. Of course, I sometimes ¹⁰ _____ nothing but I ¹¹ _____ out more than I ¹² _____ in!

Grammar

Present simple and present continuous

3 (✻) Match the sentences 1–4 with the correct description a–d.

1 Kate is studying a lot this week.
2 Alex plays computer games every day.
3 Mark doesn't live in England.
4 I'm doing this exercise now.

a present simple for regular activities
b present simple for things that are generally true
c present continuous for actions now
d present continuous for actions in the present period

4 (✻✻) Underline the correct form of the verbs.

1 John *plays/is playing* every Monday. He *plays/is playing* an important match at the moment.

2 Jackie *looks/is looking* after her little sister every day, but she *doesn't look/isn't looking* after her today because she's got exams.

3 Pete *doesn't drink/isn't drinking* coffee because he *doesn't like/isn't liking* it.

4 A: What *do you read/are you reading*?
B: Dracula. Usually I *don't read/am not reading* horror stories, but it's good!

5 They *go/are going* to the cinema every week. Right now they *watch/are watching* a comedy film.

5 (✻✻✻) Complete the text with the present simple or the present continuous form of the verbs below.

> get up ✓   meet   study   go   make   have
> learn   speak   watch   know   work

My life

I usually ¹_get up_ at eight o'clock on Saturdays. I ² _____ to drive at the moment and I ³ _____ my driving lesson on Saturday mornings. After that, I usually ⁴ _____ to the gym. I ⁵ _____ for my exams this term, so on Saturday afternoon, I ⁶ _____. In the evening, I ⁷ _____ my friends. At the moment, we ⁸ _____ plans for our next holiday– to Mexico! I want to go because I ⁹ _____ Spanish and I ¹⁰ _____ a lot about Mexico. In fact, I ¹¹ _____ a TV programme about Mexico right now!

Question words

6 (✱) **Complete the questions with the words below.**

> what   where   when   which   who   why
> how   what kind ✓   how much   how many

1 A: _What kind_ of music do you like?
  B: I like reggae.

2 A: _____ are you doing now?
  B: I'm doing my homework.

3 A: _____ CDs have you got?
  B: About fifty CDs.

4 A: _____ do you live?
  B: In Poland.

5 A: _____ are you looking in the dictionary?
  B: I want to check the spelling of a word.

6 A: _____ money have you got?
  B: About ten euros.

7 A: _____ does the class start?
  B: At nine o'clock.

8 A: _____ is speaking? I can't see.
  B: Jane.

9 A: _____ old are you?
  B: I'm fifteen.

10 A: _____ do you prefer, cartoons or music programmes?
   B: I like them both!

7 (✱✱✱) **Put the words in the correct order to make questions. Then answer the questions.**

1 you/do/Saturdays/get up/on/when

   When do you get up on Saturdays?
   I get up at ...

2 you/what/reading/at the moment/are

   _____?
   _____

3 money/do/how much/usually/you/every week/spend

   _____?
   _____

4 is/who/your favourite/actor

   _____?
   _____

5 how many/you/sports/do/do

   _____?
   _____

6 films/you/like/what kind/of /do

   _____?
   _____

Grammar reference
Present simple and present continuous

Use of the present simple
Use the present simple to talk about:

• regular activities/habits in the present.
He **plays** football every Sunday morning.

• things that are always/generally true.
My mother **doesn't speak** German.

Use of the present continuous
Use the present continuous to talk about:

• actions at the moment of speaking.
The sun **is shining**.   (= now, as I speak)
It **isn't raining**.   (= at the moment)

• actions in the present period but not at the moment of speaking.
I**'m reading** a fantastic book.   (= in the present period, but not as I speak)

Questions and question words

• Wh- questions ask for information. The answers to wh- questions provide information and cannot have Yes or No answers.

• Meaning of wh- question words:

Question word	to ask about:
What	things
Who	people
When	times
Where	places
How	the way you do something
Why	reasons
Which	things
How many (+ noun)	a number
How much (+ noun)	quantity
How much (+ verb)	the cost of something
What time	a precise time
What kind/sort/type of	the type

• what and which:
We use both to ask about things, but we only use which if the number of answers is limited:
What do you want to do tonight?   (= unlimited number of answers)
Which film do you want to see – the Brad Pitt one, or the horror film?   (= limited number of answers)

• Word order in wh- questions:
After wh- question words, the auxiliary verb (or the verb to be) comes before the subject:

Question word(s)	auxiliary or to be	subject	rest of sentence
Where	do	you	come from?
What time	does	your	mother get home?
What	is	his	name?

Vocabulary

Talking teenagers

1 Complete the sentences with the words below.

> complain   sense of humour ✓   media
> exam pressure   appearance   support

1 Simon always makes me laugh. He has a good
   <u>sense of humour</u>.
2 Many teenagers worry about their _____ .
   They don't like the way they look.
3 I never _____ about my parents. They give
   me enough freedom.
4 My friends are great. They always _____
   me when I have a problem.
5 There is a lot of _____ at school. There
   are tests and exams every month.
6 The _____ don't usually show good
   things about teenagers.

Family and relationships

2 Complete the table with the words below.

> brother ✓ grandfather son great-grandfather
> great-grandmother step-father aunt
> husband uncle sister ✓ niece wife
> daughter-in-law nephew mother

Male	Female
brother	sister

```
                Effie ┬ Ted
                      │
        Ina ┬ Ronald      Aileen ┬ Tom
            │                    │
  Sandra   Brian    Lisa  Simon  ME ┬ Rob
                                    │
                              Ellen  Daniel
```

3 Look at the family tree. Complete the sentences
with words from exercise 2.

1 Effie is Ellen's <u>great-grandmother</u>.
2 Ronald is my _____ .
3 Rob is my _____ .
4 Daniel is Simon's _____ .
5 Ina is Effie and Ted's _____ .
6 Ellen is Lisa's _____ .
7 Ted is Daniel's _____ .
8 Aileen is Tom's _____ .

4 Answer the questions.

1 Are you an only child?
   _____
2 How often do you see your relatives?
   _____
3 How many cousins have you got?
   _____
4 Do you have any grandparents?
   _____
5 Do you have any brothers or sisters?
   _____
6 Do any of your friends have a step-father
   or step-mother?
   _____

Reading

5 Look at the photo on page 7 and the title of the
text. Choose the correct answer.

1 The two girls are
a in an office.   b at school.
2 They are
a working.   b having fun.

6 Read the dictionary extracts and the text about
teenagers on page 7. Match questions 1–6 with
the paragraph where you find the answer. Then
answer the questions.

hotline *n* special telephone line for information
or help

expert *n* someone who has a lot of knowledge
about something

advice *n* helpful information

1 ☐ How old are the teenagers who answer the
   calls? _____
2 ☐ Why do teenagers call the hotline?
   _____
3 ☐ Does the hotline help with homework?
   _____
4 ☐ What is the biggest problem for
   teenagers? _____
5 ☐ Adults sometimes call the hotline. Who are
   they? _____
6 ☐ How many hotline helpers are there?
   _____

Teens Talking to Teens

1 Tina and Jana, two high school students, are chatting when the phone rings. Jana answers, 'This is *Teens Talking to Teens*.' All this is happening in Ljubljana, the capital of Slovenia, at the Young People's Support Centre. Young people in the city help at a telephone hotline for teenagers with problems. What's so special about this hotline? Well, the people who answer the phones are fourteen to eighteen-year-olds. They aren't experts but they try to help. Two teenagers work every day from 3 p.m. to 5 p.m. They don't work at weekends or during holidays.

2 Most teenagers who phone are high school students with problems. 'We have to have a sense of humour because teenagers sometimes think we'll do their homework for them,' says Jana, 'But that's not what the hotline is for. People think teenagers' lives are fun but they often worry about school, problems with parents or even trouble with the police. Teenagers today complain that their parents don't give them enough freedom. But the biggest problem is school. They worry about teachers, marks and exams, and there is a lot of exam pressure. Also, many kids are unhappy about their appearance. We listen and try to help.'

3 'We're in the media, so everybody knows our phone number,' says Tina, 'even parents. Parents sometimes call us for support when they are having problems with their teenage daughter or son. They don't know what to do. Kids call us because they find it difficult to talk to their mum or dad. Some kids even want to leave home but we ask them to think about it for a day or two. Kids listen to us because we're kids too.'

4 The fifty Slovenian teenagers love their work. 'It's really interesting to talk to other teenagers about their problems. I think all the hotline helpers are good at listening, talking and giving advice and support to people in trouble,' says Jana.

Tina and Jana in the *Teens Talking to Teens* office

7 Read the text again. Tick (✓) true or cross (✗) false.

1 ☐ The hotline is in a Support Centre in the UK.
2 ☐ Teenagers work at the hotline in the morning.
3 ☐ Hotline helpers don't work on Saturdays.
4 ☐ Today's teenagers want more freedom.
5 ☐ Teenagers worry about their school exams.
6 ☐ A lot of kids worry about the way they look.
7 ☐ Only teenagers call the hotline.
8 ☐ The hotline helpers are good at their job.

Listening

8 DJ Karen Klass is talking to Alan Lost about British teenagers' problems. Which teenage problems do you think you are going to hear about?

9 ⌑2⌑ Listen to a recording about British teenagers' problems. Choose the correct answers.

1 Where does Alan work?
a At the radio station. **b** At a hotline.
c At a school.

2 Alan is
a a teacher. **b** not a student.
c seventeen years old.

3 Alan is answering calls about problems with
a parents and teachers. **b** friends and school.
c school and teachers.

4 Some kids
a worry about their appearance all the time.
b feel they are not good at a subject.
c don't like any of their teachers.

5 Alan thinks … can support teenagers with problems.
a other students **b** only teachers
c other family members

6 Denise has a problem with her … teacher.
a English **b** Maths **c** Chemistry

Writing

Filling in a form

1 Read Kasia's application form for the Kinglee Language School. Then match the notes in boxes A–F with the correct part of the form 1–6.

> **A** Put the day of the month first, then the month, then the year.(12/06/97 OR 12/06/1997)
> On some forms you see 'DOB'. DOB = Date of birth.

> **B** Mr = a married or unmarried man.
> Mrs = a married woman.
> Ms = a married or unmarried woman (pronounced /miz/).

> **C** The *applicant* is the person filling in the form.

> **D** Write your home address as usual, but give the English words for your town/city and country. Don't translate the name of the street into English.

> **E** Forename(s) = first name(s)
> Surname = last name or family name
> Your forename(s) and surname make up your full name.

> **F** When you write addresses in the UK, put the number first, then the name, then the kind of street *24 Elm Road, 13 Mill Street, 6 Park Avenue*. Finally, put the town or city and the postcode. Notice the punctuation when you have to write an address in one line: *34 Broad Avenue, Greenwood GR21 9TY.*

2 Read the application form again. Answer the questions.

1 What is Kasia's full name?

_____

2 How long is the course she wants to do?

_____

3 Where does she want to stay?

_____

4 What is her date of birth?

_____

5 What is her phone number?

_____

6 Has she got an email address?

_____

3 Write the dates of birth for a form. Use the notes in box A to help you.

1 23rd January 1978   *23/1/1978* or *23/1/78*
2 2nd April 2007   _____
3 9th December 1996   _____
4 21st March 2008   _____
5 19th August 2001   _____

KINGLEE SCHOOL OF ENGLISH
APPLICATION FORM

TYPE OF COURSE / ACCOMMODATION WANTED

Type of course	2-week course ☐
	4-week course ☑
	3-month course ☐
Accommodation	with family ☑
	hostel ☐
	hotel ☐

¹ DETAILS OF APPLICANT

² Title	Mr Mrs (Ms)
³ Forename(s)	KASIA MARIA
Surname	KOWALSKA
Place of birth	CRACOW, POLAND
⁴ Date of birth	08/11/1992
Sex	FEMALE
Nationality	POLISH
Passport number	00055555

⁵ UK ADDRESS

House number and street	23 MARKET STREET
Town or city	LONDON
Postcode	W1E 2NB

⁶ HOME ADDRESS

House number and street	UL. KSIĐCIA JANUSZA 14
Town or city	WARSAW
Country	POLAND
Postcode	01-452

CONTACT DETAILS

| Telephone number | (+48)22 335 77 06 |
| email address | KASIA@POPMAIL.PL |

4 Write the addresses in the correct order using capital letters where necessary and the correct punctuation. Use the notes in box F to help you.

1 fenland road/NW27 2KL /65/london

65 Fenland Road, London NW27 2KL

2 606/new york/third avenue/NY 10016

_____

3 toronto/new/34/TY16 2PP /road

_____

4 6b/edinburgh/ER3 5HL/princes/street

_____

5 Complete the strategies box with the words below.

[gaps   punctuation   capital letters ✓]

Filling in a form

- Read the form carefully before you begin to fill it in.
- Use [1] *capital letters* where necessary.
- Write the date correctly.
- Check your spelling and [2] _____ .
- Fill in all [3] _____ . If you can't answer something, write n/a (= not applicable).
- Only write necessary information.

6 Use the information below and the strategies in exercise 5 to complete Kristof's application form for Kinglee School of English.

Mika Kristof
male
born: Budapest, 8th August 1990
hungarian
uk address – 25 Vine Street, Cambridge, CB2 ERL
passport number: 2078756641
65 ibusz u budapest, 00987
(+45) 20 787 5664
kristofbiro@hotmail12.com
course: 3 months
stay with a family

Speaking

Meeting and greeting

7 Complete the mini dialogues with the expressions below.

[
Hello. Nice to meet you.
Thanks, it's great to be here.
Hi! ✓   It was fine, thanks.
How do you do?   I'm fine, thanks.
]

1 A: Hello!
   B: *Hi!*

2 A: How do you do?
   B: _____

3 A: This is my sister, Helen.
   B: _____

4 A: Welcome to London!
   B: _____

5 A: How was your journey?
   B: _____

6 A: How are you?
   B: _____

KINGLEE SCHOOL OF ENGLISH
APPLICATION FORM

TYPE OF COURSE / ACCOMMODATION WANTED		
Type of course	2-week course	☐
	4-week course	☐
	3-month course	☐
Accommodation	with family	☐
	hostel	☐
	hotel	☐

DETAILS OF APPLICANT	
Title	Mr Mrs Ms
Forename(s)	
Surname	
Place of birth	
Date of birth	
Sex	
Nationality	
Passport number	

UK ADDRESS	
House number and street	
Town or city	
Postcode	

HOME ADDRESS	
House number and street	
Town or city	
Country	
Postcode	

CONTACT DETAILS	
Telephone number	
email address	

Getting to know people

8 Put the conversation between Kristof and Kasia in the correct order.

- [1] Hi! I'm Kristof.
- [ ] Me? Oh, I'm from Budapest in Hungary. Where are you staying?
- [ ] Hi, Kristof. Nice to meet you. I'm Kasia, from Poland.
- [ ] Yes, very much. It's a fantastic city. Which course are you doing?
- [4] I'm from Katowice, in the south of Poland. And you?
- [ ] I'm doing the four-week English course.
- [ ] Which part of Poland are you from?
- [ ] I'm staying with a really nice family. Are you enjoying London?

2 the greats

*	easy to do
**	a bit harder
***	extra challenge

Vocabulary

Life events

1 Match the sentence beginnings 1–6 with the endings a–f.

1 Claudia worked
2 Ellen had a happy
3 He shot
4 Kate and Lisa became
5 They refused
6 We grew up

a himself.
b to fight in the war.
c as a model for two years.
d in the USA.
e childhood.
f world champions.

2 Complete the text with the words below.

> grew up   famous   bands   refused
> depressed   was born ✓   childhood
> himself   very successful   came from

Paul Hester ¹ _was born_ in Australia in 1959. He ² _____ in Melbourne. He ³ _____ an artistic family and he had a happy ⁴ _____. He played with different teenage ⁵ _____ as the drummer. In 1984 he formed a band called Crowded House with Neil Finn and they quickly became ⁶ _____. Their most ⁷ _____ songs include *Weather with you* and *She goes on*. The band travelled a lot. Hester wasn't happy when he was away from home and he was often ⁸ _____ . Finally, he ⁹ _____ to travel again and he left the band. Sadly, he killed ¹⁰ _____ in 2005. He was only forty-six years old when he died.

Grammar

Past simple

3 (*) Put the verbs below into the correct column. Then write their past simple forms.

> grow ✓   play   become   dance   be
> move   get   marry   die   begin   think
> start   come   have

Regular verbs	Irregular verbs
	grow – grew

4 (**) Put the verbs in brackets into the correct form of the past simple.

To: jane.green@bmail34.com
From: Emily.creith@cmail43.com
Subject: **The weekend!**

Hi Jane!

I ¹_wanted_ (want) to write before, but I ² _____ (not have) time. On Friday, Clare and I ³ _____ (go) to see the new Tom Cruise film. Amy ⁴ _____ (not go) with us – she ⁵ _____ (be) busy. We ⁶ _____ (not like) the film because it ⁷ _____ (be) boring! On Saturday, I ⁸ _____ (meet) Colin and we ⁹ _____ (decide) to go for a hamburger. The hamburgers ¹⁰ _____ (be) great!

How was your weekend?

Bye!

Emily

Grammar Plus: Time phrases with *in, on, at*

5 (***) Underline the correct words to complete the sentences.

1 What did you do *at/in/<u>on</u>* your birthday?
2 Jo's family had a good time *at/in/on* Christmas.
3 House music was popular *at/in/on* the 1990s.
4 Harry and Monica went to the cinema *at/in/on* the weekend.
5 Jay arrived home *at/in/on* 10 April.
6 When did Tim get to school *at/in/on* Tuesday?

6 (✱✱) Use the verbs in brackets to complete the questions and answers.

1 A: Where _did Jim go_ (Jim/go) on Saturday evening?

   B: He _____ (go) to Mark's party.

2 A: What time _____ (you/be born)?

   B: I _____ (be born) at three o'clock in the morning.

3 A: _____ (Maria/meet) her friends on Tuesday?

   B: No, she _____ . She _____ (meet) them on Thursday.

4 A: _____ (Paul/phone) that girl from the party?

   B: Yes, he _____. He _____ (send) her a text too!

5 A: How old _____ (be/your grandparents) when they met?

   B: They _____ (be) twenty.

6 A: When _____ (Angela/start) learning Chinese?

   B: She _____ (start) six months ago.

7a (✱✱✱) Complete the sentences using the verbs in brackets.

1 Pete and Rita _met_ (meet) on holiday in Poland.

2 Jack and James _____ (become) rock stars.

3 Eddie _____ (not move) to London, he _____ (stay) in Liverpool.

4 The concert _____ (not start) at 7 p.m., it _____ (start) at 8 p.m.

5 Liz _____ (not write) one email, she _____ (write) six emails.

6 Rex and Sophie _____ (fall) in love three months ago.

b Write a question for sentences 1–6 using the verbs in brackets above.

1 Where _did Pete and Rita meet?_

2 What _____?

3 Did _____ to London?

4 What time _____?

5 How many _____?

6 When _____?

Grammar reference

Past simple

Form

	Regular and irregular verbs
+	They remember**ed** the date. He **bought** a new watch.
–	They **didn't remember** the date. He **didn't buy** a new watch.
?	**Did** they **remember** the date? **Did** he **buy** a new watch?
Short answers	Yes, they **did**./No, they **didn't**. Yes, he **did**./No, he **didn't**.

	to be
+	I/He/She/It **was** hungry. We/You/They **were** hungry.
–	I/He/She/It **was not (wasn't)** hungry. We/You/They **were not (weren't)** hungry.
?	**Was** I/he/she/it hungry? **Were** we/you/they hungry?
Short answers	Yes, I/he/she/it **was**. No, I/he/she/it **wasn't**. Yes, we/you/they **were**. No, we/you/they **weren't**.

Wh- questions

What did she **have** for lunch yesterday?

Why didn't you **come** to the party?

Spelling of regular verb forms

Add -ed to most regular verbs: watch → watch**ed**

Verbs that end with -e, add only -d: live → live**d**

Verbs that end in consonant + y, change -y to -i : marry → marr**ied**

Verbs with one syllable that end in a vowel + consonant, double the final consonant: stop → stop**ped**

Use

Use the past simple to talk about finished actions/events in the past:

I **phoned** her yesterday evening.

Time expressions

Use **in** with decades, years and months:

in the 1990s/1929/April

Use **on** with days

on Monday/21st May/your birthday

Use **at** with a specific time or a period of time:

at 11 o'clock/midnight/the weekend/Christmas

Other time expressions

yesterday (morning/afternoon), last (week/year), ten years ago, when she was little

Vocabulary

Life events

1 Find eight life event words. Look → and ↓.

s	d	r	e	n	t	r	j
c	e	a	h	y	t	t	o
h	g	h	o	u	s	e	b
o	r	c	j	k	k	a	x
o	e	n	g	a	g	e	d
l	e	f	y	l	k	z	b
a	r	g	u	m	e	n	t
m	a	r	r	i	e	d	n

2 Complete the sentences with the verbs below.

> rented   got x3 ✓   started
> left   fell   passed   had

1 I _got_ married last year.

2 Harry _____ in love with Sally.

3 Last year, I _____ a flat in the centre of Warsaw. It wasn't very expensive.

4 Mark _____ an argument with Paul yesterday.

5 Anna _____ school when she was four years old and _____ when she was eighteen.

6 I'm happy because I _____ all my exams.

7 Did you hear? Mike and Ellen _____ engaged last week.

8 Tom _____ a degree in Maths.

3 <u>Underline</u> the correct word to complete the text.

I started university ¹ _when/then_ I was seventeen years old. I got a job ² _after/later_ I left university. ³ _Then/At_ I moved to New York and started a new job. ⁴ _Then/After_ a few months I met some new friends. ⁵ _When/Then_ I changed jobs again and met Dave. We started going out ⁶ _after/later_ a few weeks. A few years ⁷ _later/in_ we got married. Our son was born ⁸ _in/at_ 1996.

Grammar

Past continuous

4 (✱✱) What were the Jones family doing at 7.30 p.m. last night? Complete the sentences with the correct form of the verbs in brackets. Then look at the pictures and tick (✓) true or cross (✗) false.

1 ✓ Craig _wasn't studying_ (not study) for his exams.

2 ☐ Craig _____ (chat) to his girlfriend on the phone.

3 ☐ Diane and Ann _____ (do) their homework.

4 ☐ Mum and Dad _____ (not cook) the dinner.

5 ☐ The food _____ (burn) on the cooker.

6 ☐ Mum _____ (watch) TV.

5 (✱✱) Look at the pictures in exercise 4 again. Complete the questions and answers with the correct form of the verbs below.

> be x2   watch   speak   play
> eat   do ✓ x3   cook   bark

1 What _was_ Mum _doing_ at 7.30 p.m. last night?
  She _was doing_ yoga.

2 What _____ Diane and Ann_____ at 7.30 p.m. last night?
  They _____ TV.

3 What _____ the dog _____ at 7.30 p.m. last night?
  It _____ because the dinner was burning.

4 _____ Dad_____ dinner at 7.30 p.m. last night?
  No, he _____. He _____ to a friend on the phone.

5 _____ the cats _____ at 7.30 p.m. last night?
  No, they _____. They _____ some food.

Past simple and past continuous

6 (✶✶) <u>Underline</u> the correct form to complete the sentences.

1 Angelina Jolie <u>met</u>/*was meeting* Brad Pitt when they *acted*/<u>were acting</u> in *Mr and Mrs Smith*.

2 It *rained*/*was raining* when I *walked*/*was walking* to school this morning.

3 What did *Joe wear*/*was Joe wearing* when you *saw*/*were seeing* him?

4 I *listened*/*was listening* to music when Kate *arrived*/*was arriving*.

5 *Did you go*/*Were you going* to the cinema last weekend?

6 What *did you do*/*were you doing* after school yesterday?

7 (✶✶) Put the verbs in brackets into the correct tense.

1 We <u>*were doing*</u> (do) our homework at 6.30 p.m. yesterday.

2 They _____ (meet) while they _____ (study) at university.

3 I _____ (not listen) when the teacher _____ (explain) the problem.

4 We _____ (see) Sue when we _____ (play) in the park.

5 When I _____ (get up) this morning it _____ (not rain).

6 What _____ (you/do) when I _____ (phone)?

7 What _____ (you/do) last weekend?

8 I _____ (not go) to school yesterday because I _____ (be) sick.

8 (✶✶✶) Complete the text with the past simple or past continuous form of the verbs below.

decide   want   meet   read   hear   be born ✓
become   discover   be x2   phone   live   go

Raul [1] <u>*was born*</u> in a small town in Spain, but he always [2] _____ to live in another country. While he [3] _____ at university he [4] _____ about a special programme for students called Erasmus. He [5] _____ to apply. He [6] _____ a book at home one day when the organisers [7] _____. Raul had a place! He [8] _____ to Edinburgh in Scotland for a year. While he [9] _____ in Edinburgh he [10] _____ a Spanish girl. He [11] _____ very surprised when he [12] _____ that she was from the same town as him! They [13] _____ good friends.

Grammar reference

Past continuous

Form

+	I/He/She/It We/You/They	was were	
−	I/He/She/It We/You/They	was not (wasn't) were not (weren't)	working yesterday.
?	**Was** I/he/she/it **Were** we/you/they		working yesterday?

Short answers	Yes, I/he/she/it **was**. No, I/he/she/it **wasn't**. Yes, we/you/they **were**. No, we/you/they **weren't**.

Wh- questions	Answers
What were you **doing** at seven o'clock?	I **was studying**.
Why were you **crying** when she came in?	I **was** sad.

Use

Use the past continuous to talk about actions or events in progress at a time in the past:

I **was watching** TV at seven o'clock yesterday evening.
At that time, my parents **were living** in New York.

Past simple and past continuous

The past simple and the past continuous are sometimes used together. The past continuous is used for the action in progress (or the background action) and the past simple for the completed action. Sentences like this usually contain *while* or *when*.

While/When I **was walking** the dog, I **dropped** my keys.
I **was watching** the TV **when** the phone **rang**.
They **got married** in 1992, **while** they **were living** in New York.

Vocabulary

Greatest Britons

1 **Look at the pictures. Write the names of the professions using the words below.**

> writer   sports person   composer   scientist   engineer   queen ✓

1 *queen*

2 _____

3 _____

4 _____

5 _____

6 _____

2 **Match the sentence beginnings 1–7 with the endings a–g.**

1 James Dean died
2 Cleopatra led
3 Einstein developed
4 Gandhi wanted
5 Newton discovered the
6 Shakespeare wrote
7 Leonardo da Vinci designed

a law of gravity.
b the theory of Relativity.
c in a car crash.
d plays and poetry.
e the helicopter.
f peace in his country.
g the army in battle.

Personal characteristics

3 **Complete the sentences with the words below.**

> talented ✓   intelligent   brave   violent
> glamorous   popular   sympathetic   famous

1 Beyoncé is a very *talented* singer and actress. She is very good.

2 Lisa was afraid, but she sang alone anyway. I think that's really _____ .

3 Einstein was really _____ – he was a great scientist.

4 Many historical figures did terrible things. They were often very _____ .

5 All the students like her. She is very _____ .

6 He is rich and successful. A few years ago nobody knew his name, now he is very _____ .

7 I think Eva Longoria is very _____ . She always wears beautiful clothes.

8 I always talk to Jim when I have a problem, he is very _____ .

Reading

4 Look at the photographs below and answer the questions. Then read the text and check your answers.

1 Who are the people in the photos and what do they do?

_____

2 What do you think they have in common?

_____

5 Read the text again and tick (✓) true or cross (✗) false.

1 ☐ All of these actors are American.

2 ☐ Keira Knightley was in *Star Wars* when she was fourteen.

3 ☐ Johnny Depp didn't always want to be a film star.

4 ☐ Johnny Depp played the drums in his band.

5 ☐ Ellen Page's parents are actors.

6 ☐ Ellen Page won an Oscar for her role in *Juno*.

6 Answer the questions.

1 How old was Keira Knightley in the film that made her famous?

_____

2 What role did Keira Knightley play in *Love Actually*?

_____

3 What was the name of Johnny Depp's first big film?

_____

4 When did Johnny Depp change his lifestyle?

_____

5 Where was Ellen Page born?

_____

6 What was the name of Ellen Page's first film?

_____

Fame!

Do you ever dream of being famous? Today, we look at three people who were rich and famous – before they were twenty-one years old!

British actress Keira Knightley started acting when she was very young. Her father is also an actor and her mother writes plays for the theatre. When Keira was fourteen, she got a part in *Star Wars*. Three years later, she played the part of Jules, a football-crazy teenager in *Bend It Like Beckham* – the film that made her really famous. The next year she was the beautiful young wife in *Love Actually*. Then in 2003 she made the first of the *Pirates of the Caribbean* films. She was nominated for lots of awards including Golden Globes and BAFTAs.

Johnny Depp wanted to be a rock star, but he became a famous film star. His family moved around the USA a lot when he was young and he wasn't always happy. He left school when he was still in his teens and played the guitar with a band called the Rock City Angels. He was in the hit television series *21 Jump Street*, but his first big film was *Nightmare on Elm Street*. When he was younger, Johnny had a lot of famous girlfriends and he often got into trouble. But when he met Vanessa Paradis, he changed his lifestyle. He now lives happily in France with Vanessa and his children.

Ellen Page was born in Nova Scotia, Canada, in 1987. Her mother is a teacher and her father is a designer. When she was only ten years old she was in a film called *Pit Pony*. Six years later, she made *Mouth to Mouth*, a film set in Europe. Her big break came in 2005 when she starred in *Hard Candy*. The critics thought her performance was fantastic. Teenagers and adults loved her next film, *Juno*, in 2007. She was nominated for an Oscar for it. Although she didn't win the award this time, she's got lots of time to win one! She still lives in Canada and has a dog called Patti.

Reading

Matching headings with paragraphs

Exam TIP

An appropriate heading of a paragraph must not be too general or too narrow.

1 Read the title and introduction to the text to find out what it is about. Which statement do you think is true, a or b?

Edmund Hillary, first man at the top of Everest, dies aged 88

Sir Edmund Hillary, the first man to climb the world's highest mountain, died on Friday the 11th of January in Auckland, New Zealand.

a The text is about Mount Everest.
b The text is about a famous man who died.

2 Read the first paragraph of the text and the three headings. Answer the questions.

1 _____

Hillary was born in New Zealand in 1919. As a boy, he was rather shy and not very good at sports. He liked adventure books. During a school trip he discovered that he enjoyed climbing. His first major climb was Mount Olivier in Mount Cook National Park in New Zealand when he was twenty. After the Second World War he started climbing in the Himalayas.

a Hillary's childhood
b His early years
c Edmund Hillary's life

Which heading:

☐ is too general – a good title for a longer text with more information not in the paragraph?

☐ is too narrow because it only tells you about some of the information in the paragraph?

☐ tells you what the whole paragraph is about?

3 Read the second paragraph. All the <u>underlined</u> words refer to the same thing. What is it? Choose the best heading a–c for this paragraph.

2 _____

Mount Everest (8,848 metres) <u>lies</u> between Tibet and Nepal. <u>It is called Chomolungma</u> by the Tibetans and <u>Sagarmatha</u> by the Nepalese. Between 1920 and 1952, twelve expeditions failed to reach <u>its top</u>.

a The Himalayas
b The first expeditions
c The mountain

4 Read the rest of the text and match headings a–d to paragraphs 3–5. There is one extra heading.

3 _____

Hillary helped prepare the climb when he took part in two practice expeditions to Everest in 1951 and 1952. Then, on the morning of May 29, 1953, he and the Nepalese climber Tenzing Norgay reached the top. Interestingly, for many years both men refused to tell which of them was the first: they always said they did it together.

4 _____

After his great success, Hillary continued to climb in the Himalayas. He also took part in expeditions to the Arctic and Antarctic. Perhaps more importantly, all his life he worked to help people in Nepal. He travelled around the world and raised money to build hospitals and schools there.

5 _____

After Hillary's death, political leaders in New Zealand described him in their speeches as 'a legend' and 'the most famous New Zealander ever'. But we should remember that Hillary described himself as 'an ordinary person with ordinary qualities'.

a After Everest
b The Arctic expedition
c New Zealand's icon?
d First at the top

Use of English

Gap fill

5 Match the words 1–7 with the correct part of speech a–g.

1 what, why, how   **a** nouns
2 while, after, and   **b** verbs
3 twin, poetry, fitness   **c** adjectives
4 take, discover, meet   **d** prepositions
5 lazy, famous   **e** verbs (-*ing* form)
6 in, on, to   **f** linking words
7 listening, reading   **g** question words

6a Read sentences 1–7. What part of speech do you need in each gap?

1 I usually _____ my friends on Saturdays. *verb*
2 I lost my pen _____ I was walking to school. _____
3 Pat writes _____ in his free time. _____
4 _____ do you want to leave school? _____
5 Mozart was a _____ musician when he was thirteen. _____
6 Helen was _____ to music in class. _____
7 I left my bag ___ the table. _____

b Complete each sentence with a word from exercise 5.

> **Exam TIP**
>
> In a gap-fill task, the word in the gap should have the correct meaning and the correct grammatical form.

7 Complete the text with the words below. There is one extra word.

> after   childhood ✓   fall   go   left   many
> married   why   sense   when   wonderful
> how

My grandfather is wonderful. He had quite a difficult ¹*childhood*. He was one of ten children. ² _____ he was just fifteen, he ³ _____ school to go to work and help his parents. He had no time to ⁴ _____ out with friends. But he did meet my grandmother and ⁵ _____ in love with her! They got ⁶ _____ when they were nineteen. ⁷ _____ that, my grandfather worked hard, but he was never miserable and had a great ⁸ _____ of humour. When he was thirty, he went back to school and then to university! He became an engineer at thirty-seven. Now he is sixty-five and he's got a ⁹ _____ personality. He never asks '¹⁰ _____ are things at school?' or 'How ¹¹ _____ A's did you get today?' We talk about football and films. I hope I'm like him when I'm sixty-five!

Speaking

Photo description

8 Read the exam task and then do the preparation exercises below.

Here is a photo of friends spending their time together. Describe the photo.

Match the possible answers below to the three questions.

> playing instruments
> three young people   at home
> three students ✓   making music
> in a college room   a group of friends
> preparing for a concert   in a bedroom

1 Who's in the photo?
   Three students _____
2 Where are they?
   _____
3 What are they doing?
   _____

> **Exam TIP**
>
> Use the present continuous tense to say what people are doing in a photo.

9 Complete the description with the verbs below in the present continuous tense.

> eat   play ✓   smile   wear   sit

The photo shows three young people, playing musical instruments. The person in the middle ¹ *is playing* the guitar. The girl ² _____ on the sofa and playing an electric guitar. The boy on the right is playing the keyboard. I think they are at home. They ³ _____ casual clothes. They ⁴ _____ . They look relaxed and happy.

Vocabulary & Grammar

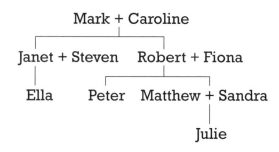

Mark + Caroline

Janet + Steven   Robert + Fiona

Ella   Peter   Matthew + Sandra

Julie

1 **Look at the family tree and complete the sentences.**

1 Mark is Caroline's _husband_.

2 Mark is Julie's _____ .

3 Fiona is Caroline's _____ .

4 Peter is Julie's _____ .

5 Ella is an _____ child.

6 Ella is Robert's _____ .

/5

2 Underline **the correct words to complete the sentences.**

1 I *play/get/on* on very well with my older sister.

2 *Glamorous/Brilliant/Brave* people are not afraid in dangerous situations.

3 Nowadays young people watch TV more often than they *play/go/do* sport.

4 I'm sure Barbara will get a place at university. She's very *determined/sympathetic/cruel*.

5 My brother *started/got/fell* engaged at twenty-three.

6 Joseph Strauss *developed/discovered/designed* the Golden Gate Bridge in 1936.

/5

3 **Complete the sentences with the correct form of the verbs in brackets. Use the present simple, present continuous, past simple or past continuous tense.**

1 Nick _reads_ (read) a lot in his free time.

2 I can't play tennis with you now. I _____ (do) my homework.

3 My father _____ (wait) for me when the plane landed.

4 In the summer we _____ (go) to the beach every day.

5 My sister _____ (not eat) meat.

6 He's a writer but he _____ (not write) anything at the moment.

7 I _____ (not see) Robert at school yesterday.

8/9 John and Susan _____ (meet) while they _____ (study) History at university.

/8

4 **Write questions for the answers. The words in bold help you.**

1 _What kind of music does she like_? She likes **rock and heavy metal**.

2 _____ ?
I'm phoning **my father**.

3 _____ ?
When you called **Fiona was having a shower**.

4 _____ ?
I've got **one sister** and **one brother**.

5 _____ ?
Ron got up at **11 a.m.** yesterday.

6 _____ ?
My boyfriend's birthday is **in August**.

7 _____ ?
On Saturday I had lunch **at home**.

/6

5 **Complete the sentences with the verbs below in the correct form.**

rent   go   have   fall   pass ✓   make   get

1 Nick's very happy. He _passed_ his last exam yesterday.

2 I can't talk to you right now. I _____ shopping.

3 His parents _____ married in 1959.

4 When I came in, my two sisters _____ an argument.

5 Many students at my university come from other towns so they often _____ a flat or house together.

6 Tom _____ in love with a Spanish girl when he was on holiday in Madrid.

7 Hannah, we _____ plans for the weekend. Where would you like to go?

/6

Reading

6 Read Cassie's article for a website for teenagers. Put sentences a–g in the correct place in the text.

  a I'm sure most of it came from your parents.

  b But there are some things that make me very angry.

  c You think they sometimes treat you like a child.

  d Do you try to understand them?

  e I think my friends don't know what they're saying!

  f They probably do more for you than you realise!

  g If you don't think they are always there for you, ask yourself some questions.

/7

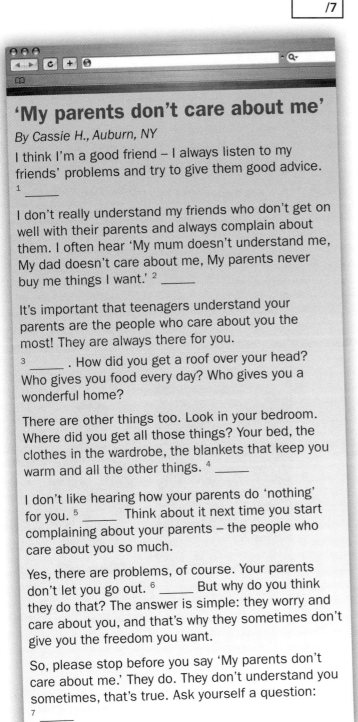

'My parents don't care about me'

By Cassie H., Auburn, NY

I think I'm a good friend – I always listen to my friends' problems and try to give them good advice. ¹ _____

I don't really understand my friends who don't get on well with their parents and always complain about them. I often hear 'My mum doesn't understand me, My dad doesn't care about me, My parents never buy me things I want.' ² _____

It's important that teenagers understand your parents are the people who care about you the most! They are always there for you.

³ _____ . How did you get a roof over your head? Who gives you food every day? Who gives you a wonderful home?

There are other things too. Look in your bedroom. Where did you get all those things? Your bed, the clothes in the wardrobe, the blankets that keep you warm and all the other things. ⁴ _____

I don't like hearing how your parents do 'nothing' for you. ⁵ _____ Think about it next time you start complaining about your parents – the people who care about you so much.

Yes, there are problems, of course. Your parents don't let you go out. ⁶ _____ But why do you think they do that? The answer is simple: they worry and care about you, and that's why they sometimes don't give you the freedom you want.

So, please stop before you say 'My parents don't care about me.' They do. They don't understand you sometimes, that's true. Ask yourself a question:

⁷ _____

Listening

7 ③ Listen to two teenagers talking on a phone-in show about people they admire. Tick (✓) true or cross (✗) false.

  1 ☐ The phone-in show is broadcast on Thursday mornings.

  2 ☐ Sally was born on 20 May.

  3 ☐ Both Sally and Kylie Minogue are the oldest of three children.

  4 ☐ Sally wants to be a professional singer.

  5 ☐ Brian had to read *A Brief History of Time* for school.

  6 ☐ Brian didn't understand everything he read on Stephen Hawking's web pages.

/6

Communication

8 Match phrases 1–8 with phrases a–h.

  1 Which course are you doing?

  2 Let me introduce you. This is my brother Tom.

  3 Where are you from?

  4 Great to see you again! Welcome to Paris.

  5 Where are you staying?

  6 How was your journey?

  7 Are you enjoying Madrid?

  8 Are you a new student too?

  a Thanks, it's great to be here!

  b Yes, I'm doing a Business course. And you?

  c Spain. How about you?

  d Nice to meet you.

  e Yes, it's cool!

  f In a student hostel.

  g Maths. How about you?

  h It was fine but a bit too long.

/7 marks

Marks

Vocabulary & Grammar	/30 marks
Reading	/7 marks
Listening	/6 marks
Communication	/7 marks
Total:	/50 marks

3 your style

easy to do
a bit harder
extra challenge

Vocabulary

Describing a place

1 Write the adjectives next to the correct picture.

[tidy   well-organised   bright   stylish
dark   messy   comfortable ✓   modern]

comfortable
_____
_____

_____
_____
_____
_____
_____

2 Complete the text with the words below. Which room in exercise 1 is it?

[bright   quiet   middle of   tidy   on
comfortable   next to   messy   noisy ✓
stylish   dark   it looks]

What kind of person are you?

Do you like ¹_noisy_ rock music or do you prefer
²_____ music? Whatever your style, your bedroom
probably says a lot about you. My bedroom has two
big windows, so it's ³_____ – that's good because
I don't like ⁴_____ rooms! I don't like ⁵_____ rooms
because you can't find anything so my room's always
very ⁶_____ . In the ⁷_____ the room there's a
rug and there's a small cupboard ⁸_____ the
bed. There's a poster ⁹_____ the wall, ¹⁰_____
very modern. I think my room is very ¹¹_____ – it
shows my style anyway! My friends say it isn't very
¹²_____ , but I don't mind.

Grammar

Comparatives and superlatives

3 Complete the sentences with the comparative form of the adjectives in brackets.

1 Sam's room is _messier_ (messy) than my room, but it's _____ (tidy) than Tom's room.

2 John is _____ (old) than Mark, but _____ (young) than Simon.

3 My French is _____ (bad) than my Spanish, but my Spanish is _____ (good) than my German.

4 I think this album is _____ (interesting) than the last one, but it's _____ (boring) than the first one.

5 These shoes are _____ (comfortable) than my blue shoes, but not as _____ (comfortable) as my boots.

4 Read about the two sisters. Complete the sentences with _not as … as_ and the correct adjective.

Hi! I'm Sarah and I'm sixteen. I'm quite tall and I always wear colourful clothes. My room is messy but that's because I'm a creative person. My friends all say that I'm not very organised and that I talk a lot!

I'm Sarah's sister, Tanya. I'm twenty and I'm not very tall. I don't like colourful clothes. I'm very organised so my room is tidy, but I'm not very creative. My friends say I'm usually quiet, but I'm very friendly.

1 Sarah is _not as old as_ (old/young) Tanya.

2 Tanya is _____ (organised/messy) Sarah.

3 Tanya is _____ (creative/well-organised) Sarah.

4 Tanya is _____ (quiet/noisy) Sarah.

5 Tanya's clothes are _____ (colourful/dull) Tanya's clothes.

6 Sarah's room is _____ (messy/tidy) Tanya's.

20

5 (✱) Complete the sentences with the superlative form of the adjective in brackets.

1 Alex is _the best_ (good) student in his class, but Mark is _____ (bad).

2 The kitchen is _____ (comfortable) room in our house.

3 These are _____ (bright) cushions I could find.

4 The bathroom is _____ (small) and _____ (dark) room in the house.

5 Kate is _____ (tidy) person in her family and Sue is _____ (messy).

6 (✱✱) Underline the correct words to complete the sentences.

1 Oliver's room is big/bigger/the biggest than my room, but Sally has got big/ bigger/the biggest room in the house.

2 Who is messy/messier/the messiest person in your family?

3 The people in the new café are very friendly/ friendlier/the friendliest.

4 Jane's clothes are very bright/ brighter/the brightest, but they're not as bright/brighter/brightest as Maggie's clothes.

5 My new phone is good/better/the best present I got this year.

7 (✱✱✱) Complete the email with the correct form of the adjectives.

To: Mark12Hawkins@hmail.com
From: Jess3Bagley@kmail.com

Hi Mark,

How are you? My family moved house this year. We were in a flat before but now we live in a house. Our house is ¹ _the smallest_ (small) in the street but not ² _____ (cheap). Its style is ³ _____ (modern) because it's ⁴ _____ (new). Our flat was ⁵ _____ (noisy) than our house because we had neighbours below us. The street is also ⁶ _____ (quiet). The bedrooms in our new house are not as ⁷ _____ (large) as the ones in the flat but there are more of them. I've got ⁸ _____ (big) bedroom in the house, all the other bedrooms are small. Our house is ⁹ _____ (far) from the road, but it's got the ¹⁰ _____ (good) view of all the houses!

I hope you can come and visit us this summer.

Best wishes,

Jessica

Grammar reference

Comparatives and superlatives

Form

	Adjectives	Comparatives	Superlatives
One syllable	long big	longer bigger	the longest the biggest
Two or more syllables	popular modern	more popular more modern	the most popular the most modern
Ending in -y	lazy friendly	lazier friendlier	the laziest the friendliest
Irregular	good bad far	better worse further	the best the worst the furthest

Use of comparative adjectives

Use the comparative form of the adjective to compare two things, people or groups of things or people. When you make comparisons using the comparative form, add _than_ after the adjective.

He is **nicer than** his sister.
Their house was **more modern than** ours.

We can also compare things using _(not) as … as_:

This essay isn't **as good as** your last one. (= your last one was better)

> **Notice!**
> _as_ + adjective + _as_ means that two things are the same:
> _Callum's **as tall as** his dad now._ (= they are the same)

Use of superlative adjectives

Use the superlative form of the adjective when you want to compare more than two things, people or groups. When you make comparisons using the superlative form, add _the_ before the adjective.

He was **the nicest** person in the school.
This is **the most modern** house in the street.

Vocabulary

Describing personal style

1 Rearrange the letters to make words describing personal style.

1 _Baggy_ (gagyb) trousers don't fit your body closely.

2 I only wear _____ (kema-pu) when I go to parties or on other special occasions.

3 Jane has got brown hair, but it's pink at the moment – it's _____ (eydd).

4 He always wears suits and he looks _____ (wlle-rddsese).

5 _____ (tgtih) clothes fit your body very closely.

6 I like _____ (saualc) clothes because I feel more relaxed.

2 Complete the descriptions of the three people with the words below.

> piercings   short x2   jewellery   straight
> long   smart   tattoo   baggy ✓   casual
> well-dressed   make-up   tight   dyed

1

He's wearing [1] _baggy_ trousers, they are quite [2] _____ too – they don't go down to his shoes. He's got [3] _____ hair. He's got a [4] _____ on one arm. His clothes style is [5] _____.

2

She's got [1] _____ hair and she's wearing lots of [2] _____ . Her skirt is [3] _____ . She's wearing lots of [4] _____ , for example, big earrings. She's got [5] _____ in her eyebrows and nose.

3

She's got long [1] _____ hair. She's wearing [2] _____ clothes – a suit and a shirt – and she's [3] _____ .

Grammar

Grammar Plus: Countable, uncountable and plural nouns

3 (*) Complete the table with the nouns below.

> money ✓   time   poster   skirt   chairs
> people   water   plants   mirror   table
> bedrooms   space

Countable singular	Countable plural	Uncountable
		money

Too much, too many

4 (*) Complete the sentences with *too much* or *too many*.

1 I've got _too much_ homework today!

2 She's wearing _____ make-up.

3 I spent _____ money last week.

4 I've got _____ shoes, I can't close my wardrobe!

5 He's got _____ cushions on his bed.

6 There's _____ space in the coffee bar. We need some more tables.

5 (**) Celia and Mike are getting ready for their party. Complete the dialogue with *too much*, *too many* or *not enough*.

C: Oh, no! There are [1] _not enough_ chairs. Twenty people are coming to the party, but we've only got fifteen chairs.

M: Don't worry. Kate and Tom can bring some chairs. Oh, I bought lots of bread.

C: Me too! I bought a lot of bread! That means we've got [2] _____ bread …, but everyone likes bread … Did you buy cheese?

M: Cheese? No.

C: Then there is [3] _____ cheese. There's only one small piece.

M: Ah, here's the lemons. I bought twenty.

C: Twenty? That's [4] _____ ! I only need two!

M: And I got one kilo of sugar for the cake.

C: I need two, so there is [5] _____ sugar!

M: Okay, I'm going to the supermarket to get sugar and cheese.

C: Great! Don't buy [6] _____ !

6 (✱✱) **What's the problem? Look at the pictures and complete the sentences with *too* or *not enough* and the adjectives in brackets.**

1 He's *not tall enough* (tall)

2 He's *too short.* (short)

3 His T-shirt is _____ . (long)

4 His T-shirt is _____ . (short)

5 Her trousers are _____ . (long)

6 Her trousers are _____ . (short)

7 Her trousers are _____ . (big)

8 He's _____ . (tall).

9 The door is _____ . (low)

10 The door is _____ . (high)

Too and *not enough* with infinitive + *to*

7 (✱✱) **Complete the sentences with *not* + adjective + *enough* or *too* + adjective and the adjectives in brackets.**

1 A: I want to play football this year.
   B: Sorry, the team is for fourteen–sixteen year olds and you're seventeen. You're *too old to be* (old/be) on the school team.

2 A: Can Tara drive?
   B: No, she's only sixteen. She's _____ (old/drive) until next year.

3 A: Do you want to go for a walk?
   B: Not today. It's 40°C, it's _____ (hot/go) outside.

4 A: Rose looks great in that dress.
   B: But she's only eleven! I think she's _____ (young/wear) those clothes.

5 A: Don't you need to get ready for the party?
   B: Yes, but I'm _____ (tired/change) my clothes.

Grammar reference

Countable and uncountable nouns

Countable nouns are things we can count, for example one table, two tables. They can be singular or plural:
*I like **parties**. I'm going to **a party** tonight.*

Uncountable nouns are things we cannot count, for example water, rice, time. They have no plural form. We cannot use *a/an* with uncountable nouns:
*I like **rice**. I'm going to buy **some rice** today.*

Too and *enough*

Too means more than the right number/amount. It is used before:
• adjectives
   *I think his trousers are **too big**.*

• *much* (with uncountable nouns) and *many* (with countable nouns in the plural)
   *She wears **too much** make-up.*
   (= her make-up doesn't look nice)
   *I've got **too many** things in my wardrobe.*
   (= it's over-full)

Not ... enough means less than the right amount. It is used before:

• adjectives
   *That jumper isn't **long enough**.*

• uncountable and countable nouns
   *I **didn't** have **enough** time in the exam.*
   (= I needed more time)
   *I **haven't** got **enough** winter clothes.*
   (= I need more winter clothes)

> **Notice!**
> The word *enough* goes before nouns, but after adjectives:
> *We didn't have **enough food**.*
> *This essay isn't **good enough**.*

You can also use *too/not enough* followed by an infinitive with *to*:
*My grandmother's **too** old **to** go skiing.*
(= she can't go skiing because she is too old)

*The girl isn't old **enough to** drive a car.*
(= the girl can't drive a car because she's too young)

Vocabulary

Money and spending

1 Match a word from column A with its opposite word in column B.

A   B

1 save   a sell

2 borrow   b mean

3 generous   c spend

4 buy   d saver

5 spender   e lend

2 <u>Underline</u> the correct words to complete the sentences.

1 Jan likes *giving/lending/earning* presents to other people.

2 I can't *save/afford/spend* a mobile phone at the moment.

3 Mia is *buying/owing/saving* some money for her summer holiday.

4 We got some great *bargains/spenders/savers* at the market this morning.

5 Maria is very *generous/mean/sensible*. She always buys her friends food at the café.

6 Can you *borrow/lend/earn* me your MP3 player, please? I'll give it back to you this evening.

3 Complete the text with the words below.

> borrow earn saver lent ✓ afford
> saved buy sensible spend paid back

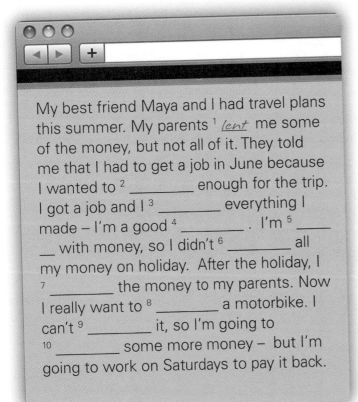

My best friend Maya and I had travel plans this summer. My parents ¹ *lent* me some of the money, but not all of it. They told me that I had to get a job in June because I wanted to ² _____ enough for the trip. I got a job and I ³ _____ everything I made – I'm a good ⁴ _____ . I'm ⁵ ____ _ with money, so I didn't ⁶ _____ all my money on holiday. After the holiday, I ⁷ _____ the money to my parents. Now I really want to ⁸ _____ a motorbike. I can't ⁹ _____ it, so I'm going to ¹⁰ _____ some more money – but I'm going to work on Saturdays to pay it back.

Listening

4 (4) Listen to the interview with successful business woman, Alina Morris. Tick (✓) true or cross (✗) false.

1 ☐ Alina's business is called Style Help.

2 ☐ Alina wasn't very interested in fashion at school.

3 ☐ Alina sometimes helps customers plan shopping trips.

4 ☐ Alina's teacher didn't think her plan was possible.

5 ☐ Alina's business became successful after only three months.

5 (4) Listen to the interview again and choose the correct answers.

1 Alina helps people to choose

a furniture/clothes.

b good styles.

c the best shops.

2 Alina wrote her business plan

a after she saw a TV programme about it.

b as part of a school project.

c in her economics class.

3 How did Alina get the money to start her business?

a She borrowed it from the bank.

b The school gave money to start the project.

c Her parents lent her the money.

4 To get new customers, Alina

a developed a website with information about Style Help.

b sent emails to a hundred people.

c asked her friends to tell people.

5 Alina thinks the most important thing is to

a have a business plan.

b start with as much money as possible.

c invest in other businesses.

Reading

6 Match questions 1–6 to the correct paragraph A–F in the text, where you find the answer to the question. Then answer the questions.

1 ☐ What can you do if you don't like working inside?

_____

2 ☐ How much money can you earn from giving classes to other students?

_____

3 ☐ Why can you save money by working in a shop?

_____

4 ☐ Why can volunteering help you get a job?

_____

5 ☐ What two animals do they talk about?

_____

6 ☐ How can you make money from creating websites?

_____

7 Read the text again. Tick (✓) true or cross (✗) false.

1 ☐ Young people can do a lot of different jobs.

2 ☐ You can earn money by taking dogs for walks.

3 ☐ Usually you can earn more than five euros for helping with studies.

4 ☐ It's possible to find work in parks in your town.

5 ☐ All shops give discounts to people who work for them.

6 ☐ You can't make much money from creating websites.

7 ☐ Volunteers sometimes earn some money.

Teens and money

So, you can't afford to go out with your friends, and you can't borrow any more money from your parents and you even owe money to your little brother. You need to get a job and earn some money! Don't worry, there are many jobs you can find or create. Here are just some ideas …

A Looking after pets

When your neighbours go on holiday, you can take care of their cat or dog or whatever pet they have. You give the animals food and exercise. Also, many people work long hours and they will pay you to visit their pets during the day and take them for a walk.

B Helping with studies

Some teens say they earn between five and twenty euros an hour tutoring. Are you good at a subject, for example, Maths or English? Then you can earn money by helping others understand it too.

C Outdoor jobs

Do you hate working inside? Don't worry – find out if there's a job in a park near your house. Often parks employ young people to collect litter or help with cutting the grass and looking after plants. You can cut the grass or clear the snow for your neighbours, too.

D Department stores

Working in a shop can be fun – and you can save money too. Some shops often give employees 20–30 percent discount on clothes and other things, so when you buy things from the shop it's cheaper for you.

E Create websites

Are you good with computers? Could you learn to create well-organised websites? Yes? Then you can make a lot of money! Some businesses pay you to create and look after their websites – doing things like adding new information and solving problems on the websites.

F Getting experience

Think about volunteering, too. Volunteers don't earn any money, but volunteering can help you get a job later. Think of a skill you want to learn or a business that interests you, then find an organisation that does it. You will get great experience doing a job there. For example, you can volunteer at a hospital. That's a great idea for students who want to be doctors. Do you like working with children? Why not volunteer to help at a local school? It's up to you to find a place that will help you learn.

Writing

Writing an email or informal letter

1 Read the email from Zack to Lily and answer the questions.

1 How does Zack start the email?

_____

2 How does Zack ask how things are?

_____

3 Who does Zack describe in paragraph 2?

_____

4 Why doesn't Zack want to miss his class?

_____

2 Complete the table with the phrases below. Then add any other phrases from the email and notes in exercise 1.

[Hi! ✓   Dear Jackie,   Hi Sarah,   Take care,
Lots of love,   Hi there!   Love,   Best wishes,]

Starting	Signing off
_Hi!_	

3 Underline the words *and, but, because* and *so* in Zack's email. Then match the words 1–4 in column A with their use a–d in column B.

A	B
1 We use *so* to	a contrast ideas.
2 We use *because* to	b link similar ideas.
3 We use *but* to	c give a reason.
4 We use *and* to	d talk about a result.

---

1 Give your email a title.

2 Open the email with *Hi* + first name if you know the person well. You can also use *Dear* + first name: … *Dear Zack,* … Don't forget the comma (,) after the name.

3 Ask how things are. Use an informal phrase: *How are you? How are things? How are you doing? Hope you're well.*

4 Say how things are: *I'm enjoying the course … Everything's going really well here … I'm really busy at the moment …*

5 In emails to friends you often use exclamation marks (!) for emphasis: *Write soon! I'm having a great time! Things are really busy here!*

6 End the email with the correct phrase: *I must go now … Please write soon … I'll email soon …*

7 Sign off with a finishing phrase and your name: *Take care, Write soon! Love, Zack. All my love, Dad Lots of love, Lisa All the best, Kev Cheers, Sam.*

To: lilyhall@hotmail2.com
From: zackjg192@1hotmail2.com
Subject: **Visit to London**

Hi Lily,

How are you? Hope you're well. Mum wrote to me and said she saw you in town. She told me that you're coming to London next month. That's great! Where are you staying? My mother's friend, Fran, says you can stay here if you want, but if you have other plans that's fine.

Everything's fine here. College is very busy! I like my roommate. His name's David and he's from Edinburgh. He plays basketball too, so we go to the sports centre together to play.

I've got to run now, it's time for my English class. I can't miss it because I've got a vocabulary exam later this week. Can't wait to see you in London!

See you soon,

Zack

4 Add *and*, *but*, *so* or *because* to each sentence to make a complete sentence.

1 I'm doing a course. I'm here for three months.

   I'm doing a course, so I'm here for three months.

2 I came to the UK. I want to study English.

   _____

3 The course is great. I'm meeting a lot of new friends.

   _____

4 I didn't want to live in a hostel. I decided to stay with a family.

   _____

5 I'm staying in London. I want to visit other English cities too.

   _____

5 Read Klara's email and tick (✓) true or cross (✗) false.

> **To:** dan@12hotmail.com
> **From:** klara@gemail29.com
> **Subject: news**
>
> Dear Dan,
> How are you? I hope that you are well. [1] I want to hear all about your course. [2] There are no problems here, things are okay. I am very busy at school. I am going to a concert tomorrow. [3] I haven't got any more news. [4] I really want to see you. Write soon. [5] I want to hear about what you're doing.
> Klara

1 ☐ She divides the email into paragraphs.
2 ☐ She doesn't use short forms.
3 ☐ She uses informal email expressions.
4 ☐ She signs off correctly.
5 ☐ She uses exclamation marks for emphasis.
6 ☐ She doesn't use conjunctions (*and, but, because, so*) to make her writing more interesting.

6a Read Klara's email again and match the <u>underlined</u> expressions 1–5 with the informal email expressions a–e.

a ☐ How's the course going?
b ☐ I think that's everything.
c ☐ I miss you all!
d ☐ Everything's fine here.
e ☐ I'd love to hear all your news.

b Write Klara's email from exercise 5 correctly.

7 Complete the strategies box with the words below.

[title   say   sign off   to ✓   from]

An email letter

- Remember to write who the email is [1] *to* and [2] _____ .
- Give the email a [3] _____ in the subject line.
- Use appropriate phrases to open the letter, ask or [4] _____ how things are, end the email and [5] _____ .
- Use *and, but, because* and *so* to write longer sentences and make your email more interesting.

8 Read the task and then write your email. Use the strategies in exercise 7 to help you.

> You are doing a language course in the UK and staying with a family. Email your British friend and inform him/her:
> - why you are in the UK and where you are staying
> - about the course and your new friends at the language school
> - how long you are going to stay and that you hope to see him/her next week.

Speaking

Going shopping

9 Complete the dialogue between Julie (J) and a shop assistant (A) with the phrases below.

[try it on   pay by card   fitting room
What size ✓   Medium   receipt
a bigger size   enter your PIN number]

Assistant: Hi. Can I help you?

Julie: Yes, I'm looking for a party dress. Do you have anything in red?

A: [1] *What size* are you looking for?

J: [2] _____ , please.

A: What about this one?

J: It's lovely. Can I [3] _____ ?

A: Yes, of course. The [4] _____ is over there.

J: It's too small. Could I have [5] _____ ?

A: Here you are.

J: It's perfect. Is it okay if I [6] _____ ?

A: Sure, no problem. Can you [7] _____ , please?

J: Sure.

A: Here's your [8] _____ . Enjoy the party!

4 your goals

✳	easy to do
✳✳	a bit harder
✳✳✳	extra challenge

Vocabulary

Education

1 Match a verb from column A with a noun from column B.

A		B	
1	drop	a	an exam
2	take	b	a subject
3	pass	c	a foreign language
4	go to	d	an exam
5	study	e	good marks
6	get	f	secondary school

2 Complete the text with the words below.

> GCSE exams   mixed schools ✓   marks
> single-sex schools   high school students
> course   A-levels   university   compulsory

School in the UK

In Britain, most students go to [1] _mixed schools_ with boys and girls in the same class, but some students go to [2] _____. It's [3] _____ to study Maths, English and a foreign language. You take your [4] _____ when you are sixteen years old and your [5] _____ when you are eighteen years old. After that, if you want, you can go to [6] _____. If you want to do a popular [7] _____ like Law or Psychology, you need good [8] _____ in your exams. In the USA, [9] _____ can study practical subjects like driving too.

Grammar

Wishes and intentions

3 ✳ Use the prompts to make sentences with *going to* and *planning to*.

1 Ian/plan/be a journalist
   Ian is planning to be a journalist.

2 we/not go to/study/French
   _____

3 I/go to/have a gap year
   _____

4 Mark and Simon/plan/go to Italy
   _____

5 she/not plan/do Art
   _____

6 they/go to/go to university
   _____

4 ✳ Complete the sentences with the correct form of the verbs in brackets.

1 James _would like to be_ (would like/be) a lawyer.
2 Kate _____ (want/study) Art at university.
3 We _____ (would like/learn) another skill.
4 John _____ (not want/have) a gap year.
5 They _____ (not want/go) to university.

5 ✳✳ Put the words in the correct order to make questions.

1 planning to/go/to/you/university/are ?
   Are you planning to go to university?
   Yes, I am.

2 you/what/going to/study/are ?
   _____
   _____

3 have/like to /would/you/a gap year ?
   _____
   _____

4 English/are/planning to/use/in the future/you ?
   _____
   _____

5 would/visit/like to/you/where ?
   _____
   _____

6 be/want to/do/in the future/you/what ?
   _____
   _____

6 (✷✷) **Read about Martin's plans and wishes for the next few years and make sentences.**

Intentions

travel for three months ✓

not go straight to university

have a gap year

Wishes

travel around Asia ✓

work for a charity organisation

study Geography at university

1 *He's going to/planning to travel for three months.*

2 *He wants to/He'd like to travel around Asia.*

3 _____

4 _____

5 _____

6 _____

7 (✷✷✷) **Complete the dialogue between Danny (D) and his French friend, Simone (S) with the correct form of *going to* or *would like* and the verbs in brackets.**

D: Hi, Simone! I passed all my exams!

S: That's fantastic! So, what are your plans? What ¹ *are you going to do* (do) now?

D: Well, I've got a place at university next year. I ² _____ (not go) this year because I ³ _____ (take) a gap year first.

S: Oh really? What ⁴ _____ (do)?

D: Well, I'm not sure. I think I ⁵ _____ (go) to France for a few months because I ⁶ _____ (study) French at university, as you know.

S: Sounds great.

D: But I haven't got much money, so I ⁷ _____ (find) a job in France. Maybe you could help me, Simone?

S: Sure. What ⁸ _____ (do) here? Have you got any ideas?

D: Well, I'm not sure. I ⁹ _____ (work) in a bar or a shop to practise my French.

S: Great. I got a job last week, I ¹⁰ _____ (work) in a friend's shop for the summer. I'll ask if there's a job for you too.

D: That's fantastic, Simone.

S: I'll phone you next week. Bye for now.

D: Bye!

Grammar reference

Wishes and intentions

going to, planning to

We often use *going to* + infinitive to describe future intentions, either in the near or distant future:

I'm going to have a party for my birthday this year.
I'm not going to get married.

In the same way we can use *planning to* + infinitive.

She's planning to study Law.
What are you planning to study?

> **Notice!**
> We don't need to repeat the verb *go*:
> *We're not going (to go) swimming on Saturday.*

want to, would like to

Both verbs describe future wishes. They are followed by an infinitive:

***Does** she **want to go** to university?*
*They **don't want to** study abroad.*
*They**'d** (= **would**) **like to travel** next summer.*

Would like to sounds more polite than *want to* so we often use it in invitations:

***Would** you **like to come** to my party next weekend?*

> **Notice!**
> *Would like to* is often used in questions but it isn't used in the negative very much.

Vocabulary

Getting a job

1 Match the pictures 1–5 with the descriptions below.

> fill in an application form   start work   do a part-time job
> look for vacancies ✓   get a job offer

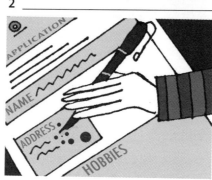

1 *look for vacancies*

2 _____

3 _____

4 _____

5 _____

2 Complete the leaflet with the words below.

> write your CV   earn some money
> an application form   adverts ✓
> go for an interview   fill in   receive

Jobs and work

Look through the ¹ *adverts* in your local newspaper or on job websites.

Make a list of all the jobs you think are interesting and then ² _____ .

If possible, phone up the companies and ask for ³ _____ .

After you ⁴ _____ an application form ask someone to check it for you.

When you ⁵ _____ wear smart clothes, it's important to look well-dressed. Remember to be on time!

When you ⁶ _____ a job offer, phone the company to accept or refuse the offer.

After you start work and ⁷ _____ it's a good idea to save some every month – don't spend it all!

Grammar

Gerunds and infinitives

3 (✱) Are the verbs below followed by a gerund or an infinitive? Put the verbs in the correct column.

> love ✓   decide   expect   spend time
> would like   want   learn   hate   enjoy
> hope   need   forget   give up   try

Gerund	Infinitive
love	

4 (✱✱) Put the verbs in brackets into the gerund or infinitive.

1 I don't mind *studying* (study) hard if it helps me to get a good job.

2 Carla expects _____ (do) well in her exams.

3 Jake doesn't like _____ (work) with numbers.

4 My friend hates _____ (write) emails.

5 Mike would love _____ (invite) Kate to the party.

6 Edward agreed _____ (write) the music for the film.

5 (**) Complete the text with the correct form of the verbs in brackets.

Hi, everyone! I'm Shannon from New York. I'm new to this website and I hope ¹ _to make_ (make) a lot of friends who like ² _____ (do) the same things as me. I love ³ _____ (draw) and ⁴ _____ (paint) and really enjoy ⁵ _____ (be) creative. I'm in my last year at school and I plan ⁶ _____ (go) to art college next year. In the future I'd like ⁷ _____ (work) as a graphic designer. I spend a lot of my free time ⁸ _____ (listen) to music from all over the world and I intend ⁹ _____ (visit) lots of countries when I start ¹⁰ _____ (earn) money.

Posted by: Shannon

6 (**) Use the verbs below to write sentences about yourself.

enjoy ✓ can't stand plan love
need don't mind

1 _I enjoy working with my hands._
2 _____
3 _____
4 _____
5 _____
6 _____

7 (***) Jackie (J) is telling her friend Alex (A) about a problem. Complete the dialogue with the correct form of the verbs below.

be teach practise learn leave ✓ help
live do employ meet speak

J: Help! My parents are driving me crazy. I want ¹ _to leave_ home.

A: What? You enjoy ² _____ with them!

J: Usually … but last month they decided ³ _____ a new nanny for my younger sister and I can't stand ⁴ _____ with her.

A: Why not? You usually love ⁵ _____ new people.

J: Well, she's Spanish and she only started ⁶ _____ English last week. Now my parents expect me ⁷ _____ her with her homework every night. I don't mind ⁸ _____ it sometimes but they want me ⁹ _____ to her all the time in English.

A: Look, you need ¹⁰ _____ your Spanish. I'm sure she wouldn't mind ¹¹ _____ you some Spanish too. You should talk to your parents.

J: Good idea, I will.

Grammar reference

Verbs with gerunds and infinitives

Verbs with infinitives

Some verbs are followed by the infinitive. Common verbs that take the infinitive are:

agree	We **agreed to meet** at 8 p.m.
decide	He **decided to apply** for the job.
forget	She **forgot to post** the letter.
expect	They **didn't expect to win**.
help	Can you **help** me **to move** it?
hope	I **hope to find** a good job.
intend	I **intended to ask** him, but I forgot.
learn	I **learnt to use** a computer.
need	You **need to know** what you want.
plan	Marta **is planning to change** jobs.
refuse	He **refused to help** them.
try	I **tried to do** the exercise, but I couldn't.
want	We **want to go** to the concert.
would love	I **would love to meet** a famous actor.
would like	I'd **like to find** a job in my town.

We usually use the infinitive after adjectives, for example: *interesting, difficult, easy.*

It's very **difficult to get** a good job without any experience.
It's **easy to travel** abroad nowadays.

Verbs with gerunds

Some verbs are followed by the gerund. Common verbs that take the gerund are:

can't stand	I **can't stand getting** up early.
dislike	She **dislikes studying** at the weekend.
don't mind	I **don't mind starting** on a low salary.
enjoy	We **enjoy doing** sport.
finish	She **finished writing** the email.
give up	He **gave up asking** her to go out with him.
hate	I **hate being** cold.
like	They **like going** to parties.
love	Mattie **loves shopping**.
miss	I **miss seeing** you every day.
stop	He **stopped reading** his book.
spend time	Amy **spends** a lot of time **reading**.

We usually use the gerund after prepositions, for example: *at, about, by.*

Are you worried **about finding** a job?
He learned English **by listening** to pop songs.

Notice!

Some verbs can be followed by the infinitive or gerund with no change of meaning, for example: *start.*

He **started learning** English when he was ten.
He **started to learn** English when he was ten.

Vocabulary

Describing jobs

1 Match the descriptions of jobs 1–6 with the words below.

> graphic designer   nanny ✓   IT consultant
> accountant   sales representative
> social worker

1 I'm good with children. I look after two children every day.   _nanny_

2 I work in a big company and look after the money.   _____

3 I work with a computer and design magazines.
_____

4 I travel a lot and sell my company's products.
_____

5 I work with different people and help them with their problems.   _____

6 I'm good with computers. I design programmes and solve problems in computer systems.   _____

2 Find six words to describe jobs.

w	d	r	g	v	x	r	y	s
e	c	e	l	h	n	s	z	t
l	r	w	a	c	x	e	a	r
l	e	a	m	s	r	c	f	e
-	a	r	o	g	w	u	o	s
p	t	d	r	o	h	r	k	s
a	i	i	o	v	y	e	w	f
i	v	n	u	y	y	p	o	u
d	e	g	s	j	d	x	k	l

3 <u>Underline</u> the correct words to complete the sentences.

1 I earned a lot of money in my last job. The _salary/application_ form was very good.

2 I'm looking for a _stressful/temporary_ job this summer. I only want to work for two months.

3 I didn't have any _experience/employers_ when I started this job, I had to learn a lot.

4 I want a creative _career/accountant_ because I love working with my hands.

5 My _employers/workers_ are great to work for. The manager is really good with people.

6 I have to work long hours and there's always too much work. My job is very _glamorous/stressful_.

7 I don't earn much money because my job isn't _rewarding/well-paid_, but I love my job!

Reading

4 Look at the web page and choose the best answer.

1 The web page is for

a employers who have jobs for students.

b students who want to take a gap year.

5 Read the dictionary extracts and the text about gap years on page 33. Match the headings a–f with the correct paragraph 1–5 in the text. There is one heading you do not need.

> **internship** _n_ In America, an internship is a job that a student does for a short time to get career related work experience

> **option** _n_ a choice you can make in a particular situation

> **placement** _n_ a job which gives you experience of a particular type of work

a What sort of programmes are there?

b What do we do?

c How often do students take part in the programmes?

d How can a gap year help me?

e What is a gap year?

f What are the jobs like?

6 Read the text again and tick (✓) true or cross (✗) false.

1 ☐ All European students now take gap years.

2 ☐ _The Center for Interim Programs_ works with one main organisation.

3 ☐ _The Center for Interim Programs_ only has information about a few study programmes.

4 ☐ It's a good way to find out what you do well.

5 ☐ You can live with a family in another country on some programmes.

6 ☐ You can earn a lot of money doing this kind of job.

Gap Year Jobs and Study Programmes

Are you finishing school and planning to go to university? If you want to get some job experience or travel, then think about taking a gap year. You'll love it!

Now, many students in Europe don't go straight to university, they take a gap year. During their gap year they travel abroad, engage in internships, study or volunteer to help others. In the United States taking this kind of time is also described as a gap year.

The Center for Interim Programs helps young people find gap year options. We work with many organisations all over the world to find placements for young people. We have information about over 5,200 options. We work with you to identify programmes that match your interests and experience.

It can help you in many ways! For most young people this is the first time they travel alone or have a job-like placement. It is a chance to grow up – and to get some great work experience. You can explore your talents and find out what you are good at – if you are good with people or with your hands, for example.

There are thousands of options to choose from! You can choose anything from cultural study programmes to job-like internships at home or abroad. We have cultural study programmes in Nepal, Ghana and Central America. You stay with a local family and study the language, history or art history of that country. We have all kinds of jobs – from working with children or animal-like placements to working in an office.

The jobs won't be too stressful because someone is there to look after you. You don't get paid for the jobs, but they are very rewarding, and you learn a lot.

Reading

True/False

Exam TIP

To decide if a sentence is true or false, look in the text for the same information in different words. Sometimes you will see a synonym of a word, an antonym or a longer phrase with the same or opposite meaning.

1 Match a word from column A with a word which means the same from column B.

A	B
1 big	a unhappy
2 depressed	b everybody
3 everyone	c large

2 Match a word from column A with a word which means the opposite from column B.

A	B
1 expensive	a dark
2 tidy	b cheap
3 bright	c messy

3 Tick (✓) the sentences that mean the same and cross (✗) the different one in each item.

1
a ✓ She's got a very big flat.
b ✓ Her flat is really large.
c ✗ Her flat is quite small.

2
a ☐ These shoes were not expensive.
b ☐ These shoes cost a lot.
c ☐ These shoes were cheap.

3
a ☐ Some people in my class like shopping.
b ☐ All the people in my class like shopping.
c ☐ Everybody in my class likes shopping.

4 Read the text and the statements 1–5. <u>Underline the words or phrases in the text which are related to each statement.</u> Tick (✓) true or cross (✗) false.

1 ☐ Smart casual clothes can be a bit messy.
2 ☐ Smart casual clothes are usually a dark colour.
3 ☐ Your shoes must not be dirty.
4 ☐ Some companies accept jeans.
5 ☐ Some people say smart casual clothes are too expensive for them.

Style Online

Every week Kathy answers your questions about fashion.

My brother Nick and I have been invited to a party at my mum's office. The invitation says 'Dress code: smart casual.' What exactly are 'smart casual' clothes? question posted by JennyD

Smart casual clothes are smarter than casual clothes but more casual than smart clothes… It is a style which shows you are relaxed, but tidy and well-dressed.

You have probably seen the clothes your parents or other adults wear to work: a suit, shirt and tie for a man, and a suit (trousers plus jacket or skirt plus jacket) and a smart blouse for a woman. These are traditional business clothes. In smart casual style a suit is not necessary, and the clothes can be brighter and more colourful.

Nick can wear good quality cotton trousers with a shirt or polo shirt plus a jacket or a smart sweater. A tie is not necessary, but clean shoes are!

Jenny – you can be quite creative. Choose a fashionable skirt or trousers with a matching top, a sweater or cardigan plus some jewellery. Don't forget a smart bag.

What's *too* casual? Mini skirts and baggy trousers are not suitable. Not all companies allow jeans, even at office parties. Jewellery is okay, but your mum's boss might not like to see piercings (except earrings) and tattoos.

Some people say they cannot afford 'smart casual' clothes! They say a suit is always a suit, even if it's cheap, but casual clothes are 'smart' only when they are fashionable designer items. But a creative teenager can spend £15 at a second-hand shop and be the best-dressed person at the party!

Listening

Note taking

Exam TIP

Before you listen always read the task carefully and think about what you might hear. This can help you to predict some of the answers.

5 Read the listening task in exercise 6. What kind of information is missing from each gap?

a an adjective
b a noun
c a number
d a date
e a word someone is going to spell

6 (5) Listen to a head teacher giving a short talk to some foreign students who want to join the school. Complete the missing information.

Rustington School

Rustington is a private [1]_____ school.

The first girls joined the school in [2]_____.

Number of students: [3]_____

Compulsory subjects for GCSE students: English, Mathematics and [4]_____

Year 10 class teacher: Miss Heather [5]_____

School uniform: [6]_____ jumper and tie, white shirt, grey trousers/skirt

---

Use of English

Gap fill: choose the correct answer

Exam TIP

In gap-fill tasks you may have to choose the right verb form, preposition, linking word, collocation or part of a fixed phrase. First look at the words *before* and *after* the gap and then *the whole sentence* to decide the correct answer.

7a Choose the best word a, b or c to complete the sentences. The <u>underlined</u> words help you.

1 I <u>can't stand</u> *c* homework on Sunday evening.

   a do   b to do   c doing

2 There's a sofa ____ <u>the middle</u> of the room.

   a on   b in   c at

3 She usually ____ smart <u>clothes</u>.

   a carries   b wears   c puts

4 I ____ some new clothes <u>last week</u>.

   a buy   b am buying   c bought

5 My room is very small, ____ I like it.

   a because   b if   c but

b What helped you choose the correct answers in exercise 7a? Match the following questions with sentences 1–5.

  a ☑ 2 What preposition do I need in this phrase?

  b ☐ Do we use a gerund or an infinitive after this verb?

  c ☐ Which word links the two parts of this sentence well?

  d ☐ Which verb can we use before this noun?

  e ☐ Is the sentence about a present or a past action?

8 Choose the best word a, b or c to complete the text. The highlighted words help you.

My dreams

My most important dream is to live in the countryside. I enjoy [1] *a* outdoors and working with animals. I [2] ____ Biology at the university now and I hope [3] ____ at a National Park in the future. At the moment I've got a part-time [4] ____ at the zoo. It's not very well-paid, but I save a little bit of money every month, [5] ____ some day I want to have a house in the country – not a very big one, but bigger [6] ____ our flat in the city. Some people think I'm crazy. They say, 'You speak foreign languages, you are good with numbers, you could [7] ____ a lot of money!' But I don't want to work long hours [8] ____ an office. I want to live in a quiet place, do what I like and be happy.

1 a being   b to be   c be

2 a studied   b was studying   c am studying

3 a working   b to work   c worked

4 a work   b job   c vacancy

5 a because   b so   c but

6 a as   b too   c than

7 a earn   b do   c spend

8 a to   b at   c in

Speaking

Guided conversation

9 Read the exam task and complete the conversation with the words below.

Look at the pictures of possible birthday presents for a friend. Talk together about the advantages and disadvantages of these ideas and decide which present to buy

[best both like looks ✓ more enough than about too]

A: So, what shall we buy for Annie?

B: How about this watch? It [1] *looks* nice.

A: I'm not sure. I like it, but I don't think it is big [2]_____ for her. You know her style.

B: True. So what do you suggest?

A: I really [3]_____ the watch.

B: I do too, but it looks [4]_____ expensive.

A: Yes, you're right. How [5]_____ the book?

B: It looks interesting. But personally, I think the CD is the [6]_____ idea. She likes pop music.

A: I think the book is [7]_____ interesting [8]_____ the CD.

B: Why don't we buy them [9]_____? They'll still be cheaper than the watch.

A: Good idea.

self-assessment test 2

Vocabulary & Grammar

1 Underline the word that you cannot use with the words in bold.

1 casual/*well-dressed*/smart **clothes**
2 tight/straight/dyed **hair**
3 owe/afford/spend **money**
4 secondary/single-sex/temporary **school**
5 part-time/compulsory/school **subject**
6 stressful/secure/mean **job**

/5

2 Complete the sentences with one word in each gap.

1 *Medicine* is one of the most popular university courses because many young people want to become doctors.
2 Could you _____ me some money, John? I'll pay you back tomorrow.
3 How many A-levels are you planning to _____ next year?
4 This is my first job so I don't have any _____ .
5 At a job _____ they always ask you about your qualifications.
6 My new dress came from a very cheap shop and only cost £10. It was a real _____ !
7 Our grandmother is very _____ . She always gives us presents and money.
8 Your hair is too _____ . Do you want me to cut it a little for you?

/7

3 Complete the gaps with the correct form of the verbs in brackets.

1 I hate *getting up* (get up) early.
2 She expects _____ (begin) work next Monday.
3 I don't mind _____ (wait) for you after school.
4 They learnt _____ (swim) when they were in primary school.
5 I'm a vegetarian and I really don't miss _____ (eat) meat.
6 Do you enjoy _____ (go) to parties?
7 Susan tried _____ (learn) Chinese but it was too difficult for her.

/6

4 Underline the correct words to complete the sentences.

1 His winter coat was much more expensive *than*/as/from mine.
2 Helen's planning work/to work/working in a big company for a few years.
3 Are/Do/Would you want to go to the cinema with us?
4 Tom's bad/worse/the worst student in our class.
5 What are you going/want/like to do after school?
6 My mum thinks I'm not enough old/enough not old/not old enough to have a piercing.
7 Would you like study/to study/studying at Oxford University?

/6

5 Complete the sentences with the comparative or superlative form of the adjectives from the box below. Add any necessary words.

[comfortable   tidy ✓   rewarding   short
baggy   messy   good]

1 My room isn't *as tidy as* my brother's.
2 Tom's quite good at Maths but I think I'm _____ with numbers than him.
3 I don't like cleaning. My mum says my bedroom's _____ room in the house.
4 I think this sweater's _____ for you. Is it your older sister's?
5 Bethany's hair is _____ Hannah's.
6 This is _____ armchair in our house.
7 I get a lot of satisfaction in my new job. My last job wasn't _____ this one.

/6

Reading

6 Read the holiday brochure and match the people 1–7 with the best place A–C for their summer holiday.

Summer Activity Ideas for Teenagers

A **Bournemouth, UK**

Are you planning to work for the radio in the future? Come to sunny Bournemouth on the south coast of England and get some experience on our amateur radio station. Our team report what's happening and play music for locals and tourists. They spend several hours each day making and broadcasting radio programmes but there's still free time to go swimming and relax. You can come to work in your shorts and go to the beach when you finish!

No experience necessary. Call 0800 222 2222 for more information. Learn about radio for only £320 for two weeks or £450 for three weeks.

B **La Esperanza, Honduras**

Want to do something different this summer? Have you ever looked after younger brothers or sisters, nieces or nephews? Come to La Esperanza and work in a local childcare centre. Our volunteers teach and play with around fourty children every day. The children are between three and nine years old and you need to give them your love and attention for twenty-four hours a day, seven days a week. The job is very rewarding but it's also hard work.

Experience necessary. Send us your CV. The minimum stay is one month. We pay for your uniform and accommodation. You only pay for travel and meals. We also offer free Spanish lessons twice a week.

C **Lancy, Switzerland**

Not sure what to do in the summer? Join us at the international camp for young people aged fourteen to eighteen in Lancy. Good German, French or English necessary. Spend time with teenagers from different countries and do some voluntary work for a local area. Can't afford to come? Don't worry. We have some vacancies for part-time jobs at the camp (Saturdays and Sundays only).

Vacancies from July (for one week to two months). Fill in and email the application form to us.

1 ☐ Paul needs a part-time job this summer.

2 ☐ Barbara has a lot of experience in babysitting.

3 ☐ Mike's only planning to go away for ten days.

4 ☐ Robert wants to get some experience for his future career.

5 ☐ Janet would like to learn a new foreign language.

6 ☐ Fiona likes wearing casual clothes.

7 ☐ Tim doesn't mind working very long hours over the summer.

/7

Communication

7 <u>Underline</u> the correct words in the first line of each dialogue. Then choose the second line from the options below.

1 A: Excuse me, do you have this jacket in a smaller *size/number*?

　B: ___d___

2 A: Can I try this dress *on/out*?

　B: _____

3 A: Can I *help/serve* you?

　B: _____

4 A: Is it okay if I *pay/buy* by credit card?

　B: _____

5 A: I think these jeans are *too/enough* small for me. Could I have a bigger size?

　B: _____

a I'm sorry but we've only got them in size ten and twelve.

b I'm just looking, thanks.

c Sure, no problem. Could you enter your PIN, please?

d Yes, are you looking for a small or a medium?

e Yes, of course. The fitting room is over there.

/8

8 Beth and Jane are at a party. Complete their dialogue with one word in each gap.

Beth: I don't know many people here. Who is that girl [1] *next* to Tom?

Jane: The one wearing the pink hat, and yellow shoes? It's his sister. She doesn't know [2] _____ about fashion – look!

Beth: Who are you talking about, Jane? [3] _____ me, her clothes are perfectly okay.

Jane: Sorry, but I don't [4] _____ with you. Yellow shoes and a pink hat? It [5] _____ weird.

Beth: Oh, come on! She's brave enough to wear what she wants. And she probably doesn't [6] _____ what people think.

/5

Marks

Vocabulary & Grammar	**/30 marks**
Reading	**/7 marks**
Communication	**/13 marks**
Total:	**/50 marks**

5 stay well

*   easy to do
** a bit harder
*** extra challenge

Vocabulary

Healthy lifestyle

1 Complete the sentences with the words below.

> cakes ready meals vegetables sleep
> soft drinks exercise fresh fruit ✓
> fast food water

1 Doctors say it's good to eat five pieces of _fresh fruit_ and _____ every day.
2 Swimming is very good _____ .
3 I try to _____ for eight hours every night.
4 We should drink two litres of _____ every day.
5 All _____ and _____ are full of sugar.
6 Pizza and hamburgers are _____ .
7 You don't have to cook _____ .

2 Underline the correct words to complete the sentences.

1 Fast food makes you _put on_/lose weight.
2 A lot of salt is _good/bad_ for your heart.
3 _Water/Sugar_ is good for your skin.
4 Cakes _contain/complain_ a lot of sugar.
5 Jane eats lots of fruit and vegetables. She has a _healthy/unhealthy_ diet.
6 Chocolate _loses/gives_ you lots of energy.

3 Complete the text about Gemma with the words below.

> fresh fruit ✓ exercise vegetables low fat
> weight sugar healthy diet sweets
> energy milk

Gemma's healthy day!

Gemma is seventeen years old and she loves gymnastics. She started classes when she was six years old. She has a big breakfast every morning. First, she has [1] _fresh fruit_ and then she has cereal with [2] _____ . This gives her the [3] _____ she needs to do a lot of [4] _____ at the gym. She trains every day and it's very important that she doesn't put on too much [5] _____ . If she needs an energy boost in the afternoon she sometimes eats a few [6] _____ because they contain a lot of [7] _____ . She eats lots of [8] _____ and drinks [9] _____ milk because it's important to her to have a [10] _____ .

Grammar

should and shouldn't

4 (*) Complete the advice with _should_ or _shouldn't_.

1 Robbie smokes three packets of cigarettes a day.
   He _should_ stop smoking.
2 Marian sleeps for ten hours every night.
   She _____ sleep so much.
3 Jenny never stays in and is doing badly at school.
   She _____ go out every night.
4 Peter has a bad heart.
   He _____ eat a lot of salt.
5 Polly can't get up in the morning.
   She _____ buy an alarm clock.
6 Colin is always hungry in the morning because he doesn't eat breakfast.
   He _____ have breakfast every morning.

must and mustn't

5 (*) Complete the text with _must_ and _mustn't_.

The Golden Rules of Climbing

Climbing is great fun, but you [1] _must_ be careful! You [2] _____ climb alone, it's dangerous, you [3] _____ climb with a partner or a group of people. You [4] _____ wear good climbing shoes and you [5] _____ use a rope. You [6] _____ climb if you feel ill and you [7] _____ eat before you climb – you need lots of energy!

should/shouldn't and must/mustn't

6 (✱) <u>Underline</u> the correct verbs to complete the text.

Football is one of the most popular games in the world – but how much do you know about it?

You ¹ _must/mustn't_ kick the ball with your foot – but you ² _should/must_ look around before you kick so you know where your team mates are! You ³ _mustn't/shouldn't_ kick other players – it's against the rules. The goalkeeper can touch the ball, but the other players ⁴ _mustn't/shouldn't_ touch the ball with their hands. You ⁵ _mustn't/shouldn't_ eat a big meal just before the game, it's not a good idea. After the game, you ⁶ _should/must_ have a shower and then relax.

7 (✱✱) Rewrite the sentences so the meaning is the same. Use _should/shouldn't_ and _must/mustn't_.

1 It's a good idea to wear comfortable shoes when you do sport.

   You _should wear comfortable shoes when you do sport._

2 It's very important to follow the rules in sport.

   You _must follow the rules in sport._

3 It's against the rules to pick up the ball in football.

   You _____.

4 It isn't a good idea to go out the night before your exams.

   You _____.

5 It's a good idea to do some exercise every day.

   You _____.

6 It's very important not to go swimming after you eat a big meal.

   You _____.

7 It's very important to have a healthy diet.

   You _____.

8 It's a good idea to sleep eight hours every night.

   You _____.

Grammar reference

should, shouldn't, must, mustn't

Form:

+	I/You/He/She/We/You/They	**must** have a good night's sleep. **should** drink a lot of water.
–	I/You/He/She/We/You/They	**must not (mustn't)** miss breakfast. **should not (shouldn't)** drive everywhere.
?	**Should**	I/you/he/she/we/you/they exercise more?
Short answers	Yes, I/you/he/she/we/you/they **should**. No, I/you/he/she/we/you/they **shouldn't**.	

Wh- questions

What should I do?
Where should we park the car?

Use of _should_ and _must_:

We use _should/shouldn't_ + infinitive (without _to_) to say that something is a good or bad idea or to give and ask for advice:

Most people **should do** more exercise.
You **shouldn't eat** too much salt.
**Should** I **take** the exam again, do you think?

We use _must/mustn't_ + infinitive (without _to_) to give strong advice or rules.

You **must** study harder to pass this exam.
Pupils **mustn't** run in the corridors.

> **Notice!**
> We don't often use _must_ in questions, except when someone is asking themselves a question:
> _What must I do?_

To ask about strong advice or rules we usually use _have to_:
Do you **have to** wear a school uniform?

Vocabulary

Food and drink

1 Add two words from the words below to each list. Can you add more words?

> apples onions pasta lemonade
> yoghurt lettuce ✓ sausages grapes
> bacon potatoes steak orange juice
> milk cornflakes cheese bananas
> milkshake chicken rice

1 You can't cook: lemonade, *lettuce*, _____
  _____

2 Good things for breakfast are: cornflakes,
  _____, _____

3 Sweet things: bananas, _____, _____

4 Good things for sandwiches are: chicken,
  _____, _____

5 Food you can eat without cooking: yoghurt,
  _____, _____

6 Your favourite food: _____, _____

2 Complete the sentences with the words below.

> bar loaf glass ✓ piece cans
> packets carton plate bottle box

1 I need a *glass* to pour my lemonade into.
2 There's a _____ of cheese on the table.
3 I bought a _____ of bread at the supermarket.
4 There are some _____ of lemonade in the fridge.
5 Can you buy a _____ of milk when you go shopping?
6 I'm having a _____ of cake with my coffee.
7 The _____ of cornflakes is on the table.
8 I had a _____ of chocolate after my lunch.
9 Can you buy two _____ of rice today, please?
10 The children have a _____ of orange juice for their breakfast.

3 Match the people 1–5 with the food and drink a–e.

1 Sam wants to have a healthy lunch.
2 Mario wants a snack and a drink.
3 Zoe needs to have breakfast in a hurry.
4 Ben is very, very thirsty.
5 Susan is in a fast food restaurant.

a some cereal with milk
b a bottle of water
c a biscuit and a milkshake
d a steak and chips
e a plate of salad and a piece of fruit

Grammar

Articles: *a/an*, *the*, zero article (Ø)

4 ✱ Complete the sentences using *a/an* or *the*.

1 Natasha is *a* Psychology student.
2 Ricky plays the piano in ___ London National Orchestra.
3 Kate would like to be ___ architect.
4 Annie is ___ secretary for ___ important business woman.
5 Ryan wants to be ___ most famous actor in ___ world.
6 Lewis works for ___ American company.

5 ✱✱ Choose the best sentence a or b for each situation.

1 You're in a bookshop. You say
a I'm looking for a book about keeping fit.
b I'm looking for the book about keeping fit.

2 You are a teacher. You say
a I work in a big school.
b I work in the big school.

3 You and your friend want to go out for a meal. You say
a I like Chinese food.
b I like the Chinese food.

4 You're in a town you don't know. You want to go out. You say
a Let's go to a disco.
b Let's go to the disco.

5 You want to catch a train. You say
a Where's nearest train station?
b Where's the nearest train station?

6 ✱✱ Underline the correct words to complete the sentences.

1 I think *the/a/Ø* diet is important for *the/a/Ø* sports stars.
2 I've got *the/an/Ø* exam tomorrow. It's in *the/a/Ø* afternoon.
3 Our science teacher says *the/a/Ø* cereals give you *the/a/Ø* energy.
4 This magazine article says that *the/a/Ø* olive oil is good for your skin.
5 We have *the/a/Ø* breakfast at 7 a.m. I have *the/a/Ø* piece of toast and *the/a/Ø* cup of tea.
6 I've got *the/a/Ø* football match after school. *The/A/Ø* match starts at 4.30 p.m.

7 (******) Complete the sentences with *a/an*, *the* or the zero article (Ø).

1 Vicky is *a* student doctor and she works in ___ small hospital.

2 Carrie is ___ English gymnast in ___ national team.

3 Paul is ___ American graphic designer and he designed ___ company's logo.

4 Ruben works for ___ multinational company and he travels all over ___ world.

5 Melanie works at ___ information desk in ___ busy airport in ___ Spain.

6 James is ___ managing director of ___ new company.

8 (*******) Read the text about Chloe and complete the gaps with *a/an*, *the* or the zero article (Ø).

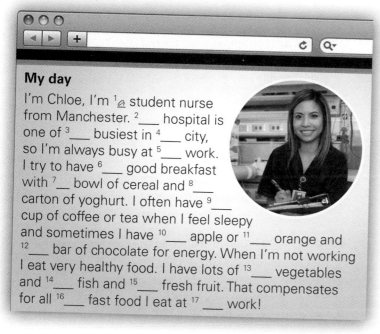

My day

I'm Chloe, I'm ¹ *a* student nurse from Manchester. ² ___ hospital is one of ³ ___ busiest in ⁴ ___ city, so I'm always busy at ⁵ ___ work. I try to have ⁶ ___ good breakfast with ⁷ ___ bowl of cereal and ⁸ ___ carton of yoghurt. I often have ⁹ ___ cup of coffee or tea when I feel sleepy and sometimes I have ¹⁰ ___ apple or ¹¹ ___ orange and ¹² ___ bar of chocolate for energy. When I'm not working I eat very healthy food. I have lots of ¹³ ___ vegetables and ¹⁴ ___ fish and ¹⁵ ___ fresh fruit. That compensates for all ¹⁶ ___ fast food I eat at ¹⁷ ___ work!

Grammar Plus: More phrases with *a*, *the* and (Ø)

9 (******) Complete the email with *a/an*, *the* or the zero article (Ø).

To: g.holloway2@bmail1.com
From: paolorosini@cmail2.com
Subject: **School in my country**

Hi Greg!

You asked about school in my country. Well, I go to ¹ *Ø* school five days ² ___ week – and I have extra classes on Saturday too! From Monday to Friday I go ³ ___ home at four o'clock. We have the best English teacher in ⁴ ___ world, she's great! We have English classes three times ⁵ ___ week. We have special 'English Days' once ⁶ ___ month too. ⁷ ___ whole class goes to the cinema to see a film in English – it's fun! We practise our English in ⁸ ___ afternoon because we talk about the film in English after.

What about your school?

Best wishes,

Paolo

Grammar reference

a/an or *the*?

We use *a/an* to talk about **one of many**.
*Neil is **a** boy in my class at school.*
(= there are many boys)

We use *the* for things that are unique – there is only one of them.
***The** president of our country lives in **the** capital city.*
(= there is only one president and only one capital city)

We only use *a/an* to talk about things **for the first time**.
*I bought **a** car a few weeks ago.*
(= the first time I talk about this car)
After that we use *the*.
*I bought **the** car from my uncle.*

a/an

We use *a/an* to:

- talk about jobs
*My mum's **an** accountant, and my dad's **a** teacher.*

- with expressions of quantity
*Would you like **a** glass of water?*
*They have **a** lot of money.*

- With these time expressions
*three times **a** day, twice **a** week*

the

We use *the* with:

- superlative adjectives
*Jo is **the** best runner in our class.*

- parts of the day
*I hate getting up in **the** morning.*

- these phrases
*in **the** world,*
***the** whole thing/day/class*

zero article Ø

We do not use articles:

- when we talk about things **in general**
Footballers shouldn't eat big meals before matches.

- when we talk about meals and meal times
I usually have breakfast at school and lunch at home.

- with phrases with *go*
go home/to school/to work

Listening

1 (6) **Listen to a TV quiz. Complete the sentences with the correct name, Jamie Anne or Bob.**

1 _____ thinks people really like chicken and steak.

2 _____ thinks the largest turkey in the world is around twenty kilogrammes.

3 _____ says it's dangerous for dogs to eat chocolate.

4 _____ is sure that Americans love peanut butter.

5 _____ is not sure when people first ate crisps.

2 (6) **Listen again and choose the correct answers.**

1 The most popular types of meat in restaurants last year were
a hamburgers, steak and beef.
b bacon, chicken and steak.
c hamburgers, chicken and beef.

2 The largest turkey ever was about … kilogrammes
a twenty.
b thirty.
c forty.

3 You need … litres of water to grow one kilogramme of rice.
a fifty
b five hundred
c 5,000

4 Americans eat almost … kilogrammes of peanuts every day.
a one million
b two million
c three million

5 People first ate crisps in
a 1753.
b 1853.
c 1953.

3 (6) **Tick (✓) true or cross (✗) false. Then listen again and check.**

1 ☐ You can eat all flowers.

2 ☐ A little chocolate is good for dogs' hearts.

3 ☐ Americans eat enough peanut butter to cover the floor of the Grand Canyon.

4 ☐ Adults eat 66 percent of the ice-cream in a typical home.

5 ☐ At the end of the quiz, Jamie has three points.

Reading

4 **Read the introduction to Helen's blog. What kind of diary is it?**

1 an exercise diary

2 a sleep diary

3 a food diary

5 **Read Helen's blog and match the missing phrases a–f to the correct place 1–6 in the text.**

a I had a cup of tea

b I cooked some bacon and eggs

c Today was a very unhealthy day

d because I was late for school

e There was nothing to eat in the fridge

f so I ate it

6 **Guess if the sentences are true or false. Then read the blog again and tick (✓) true or cross (✗) false.**

1 ☐ Monday isn't the first day of the homework diary.

2 ☐ Helen didn't eat all her cereal on Monday.

3 ☐ Helen didn't have breakfast on Tuesday.

4 ☐ Lisa had a sandwich at home with Helen for breakfast.

5 ☐ Helen had two meals on Tuesday evening.

6 ☐ The family went out for a Chinese meal on Wednesday to celebrate their dad's birthday.

7 **Read the blog again and choose the correct answers.**

1 Helen is writing the food diary
a because she's interested in biology.
b for two weeks to understand her food habits.
c because she wants to be healthier.

2 Helen didn't eat her packed lunch on Monday because
a her father made it.
b there was some cold chicken in it.
c Aziz gave her an apple.

3 Helen's favourite food is
a cereals.
b spaghetti bolognaise.
c fruit.

4 On Tuesday, Helen
a didn't eat much.
b drank a lot but didn't eat much.
c ate a lot of food but didn't drink much.

5 Lisa doesn't have breakfast at home because she doesn't
a want to.
b get up early enough.
c like breakfast.

6 On Wednesday Helen
a got up late.
b had a snack for breakfast.
c didn't have a packed lunch.

Health and Me Diary

This is my 'Health and Me' diary. It's homework for my Biology class. I have to write a diary of everything I eat and decide if it's healthy or not. I'm doing it for the next fourteen days to get a good idea of my food habits.

Monday 17 February

Well, today is the first day. I had some fruit juice and cereal for breakfast. I didn't have time to finish the cereal ¹_____. My dad made a packed lunch for me but I didn't eat it because I don't like cold chicken. Horrible! My friend Aziz gave me an apple and I ate that. I don't like fruit much, but I was hungry ²_____. Mum made my favourite dish, spaghetti bolognaise, in the evening. It was delicious.

Today's health level: *** (*Good, but eat more at lunch.*)

Tuesday 18 February

I ate a lot of food today. I was hungry ALL DAY! In the morning, I got up early and had a very big breakfast! ³_____. It was delicious! Lisa, my sister, always gets up too late to have breakfast, so she didn't have a big breakfast with me. Sometimes she has time to have an orange juice, but she never eats breakfast at home. She usually has a sandwich on the way to school! I had a bar of chocolate for elevenses. For once, my packed lunch from Dad was tasty! I ate it all because I love cheese sandwiches with tomato sauce. When I got home from school, ⁴_____ and ate two cream cakes. For tea, I made myself a pizza and, later, I had a bowl of pasta while I was watching TV.

Today's health level: ** (*Not bad, but don't eat too many sweet things. Drink more water!*)

Wednesday 19 February

⁵_____!! I didn't have any breakfast because I felt full from yesterday's food. I only had a snack at twelve o'clock because Dad got up late this morning and forgot to make my packed lunch. After school I was really, really hungry and I had a headache. ⁶_____ but luckily Dad brought home a Chinese takeaway because it was a special occasion – his birthday.

Today's health level: * (*Bad, don't miss meals.*)

Writing

An invitation

1 Read invitation A and answer the questions.

1 What is the title of the invitation?

_____

2 When and where is the event?

_____

3 What is the reason for the event?

_____

4 Who is organising the event?

_____

5 Can you take friends?

_____

6 Who do you contact if you want to go?

_____

A

DISCOVER SCOTLAND

Please come to the Discover Scotland afternoon

Don't miss the chance to try traditional Scottish food, drinks and dancing
Bring your friends and family!

**On Thursday 23 September
at 3.30 p.m.**

in the school library

The school English Club are holding an afternoon to learn all about Scotland.

If you are interested, contact Sara in class 4B

R S V P

---

1 Give the invitation a title to get people's attention: *Come to a party! Farewell Mrs. Smith,* a _School concert_

2 Ask people to come:
Please come to ...,
We'd like to invite you to ...,
I'm having a birthday party,
b _____ .
A formal invitation usually says:
We request
c _____
(= We'd like to invite you.)

3 Give the date, the time and the place. Use the correct prepositions:
from 5 till 8 at the Cat Restaurant,
d _____ .

4 Give reason for a party:
A party to celebrate ...,
An evening to learn about ...,
A party to say farewell to ...,
A welcome party for ...

5 Ask people to reply to the invitation and give a contact name, number or email:
If you want to come, contact ...
If you are interested, call ....,
RSVP (RSVP = French for 'Please reply'),
e _____ ,
f _____ .

---

2 Read invitations B and C. Add the <u>underlined</u> phrases to the examples a–f in notes 1–5 above.

B

<u>School concert</u>

Dear Parent:
The Headmaster, staff and students of
Smithills Secondary School
request <u>the pleasure of your company</u>
at the music concert
<u>on June 8 2009 at 7 p.m.</u>
<u>in the school hall.</u>

Guest of Honour: The Conductor of
Manchester Orchestra

<u>RSVP The school secretary</u>

C

To:	Elizabeth Hardy
From:	Rebecca Oakley
Subject:	**School music concert**

Dear Aunt Liz,

Our school music concert is on June 8 in the school hall at 7 p.m. and I'm going to be in it. I'm playing the piano. <u>I'd really love it if you could come</u> and see it. Mum says you can stay overnight if you want. We're going out for a meal after!

<u>Please ring Mum if you can make it.</u>

Love

Becky

3 Match the sentences to the correct type of invitation A, B or C.

A Fancy dress party   **B** Traditional food party
C Farewell party

1 ☐ Please come to the Spanish Cooking evening!
2 ☐ We request the pleasure of your company at a goodbye party for James Swan.
3 ☐ We're having a party for Halloween – come in fancy dress!
4 ☐ You are invited to our party. Come as a witch or ghost!
5 ☐ Would you like to come to an evening of typical Spanish food?
6 ☐ We'd like to say goodbye to our favourite teacher.

4 Write a title for each invitation.

1 Fancy dress party   _Halloween Party!_
2 Traditional food party   _____
3 Farewell party   _____

5 Complete the sentences with the correct prepositions *on, in, from, till* or *at*.

1 We request the pleasure of your company _at_ the farewell party.
2 We're organising a summer party ___ the Sports Club ___ Wednesday.
3 Please bring nibbles because the party will go on ___ late.
4 Kira is having a birthday party ___ 16 December ___ 8 p.m.
5 Class four are celebrating the end of exams ___ 7p.m. until 11 p.m.
6 Come ___ fancy dress to the Halloween party ___ 63 South Street.

6 Complete the strategies box with the words below.

[title   unnecessary ✓   where and when]

An invitation

- Keep the invitation short.
- Don't give [1] _unnecessary_ information. Give your invitation a [2] _____ .
- Use short forms (*We're, I'd, I'm*) if you invite people you know well.
- Give enough information to make people interested.
- Give information about [3] _____ the party or event will happen.
- Remember to tell people if they must bring something (drinks, nibbles, fancy dress).

7 Read the task and then write your invitation Use the strategies in exercise 6 to help you.

You are a student on a course in the UK. You are organising an evening about traditional dishes and food from your country. You want to invite your friends from the course. Write an invitation to this event. In your invitation:

- explain what the event is about
- say where and when the event will happen
- say what dishes you're going to prepare
- write about what else will happen at the event.

Speaking

Making arrangements

8 Put the dialogue between Claire and Zoe in the correct order.

☐ Zoe: That sounds great Claire! See you on Sunday then. Bye for now.

☐ Zoe: That would be lovely. What time?

☐ Claire: Well how about Sunday afternoon instead? We can change the day if you like.

☐ Claire: Shall we all meet at my house at about 1.30 p.m?

☐ Zoe: I'm sorry, I can't. I'm going shopping for my sister's birthday present on Saturday.

1 Claire: Hi, Zoe. Are you free on Saturday afternoon? A group of us want to go horse riding.

☐ Claire: Bye, Zoe.

9 Complete the dialogues with the phrases below.

[Why don't you   Are you free   That's a good
That would be lovely   Shall we meet
Would you like to come ✓   How about
I'm afraid I've got   That sounds   I'm sorry]

1 A: _Would you like to come_ to a party on Saturday night?
   B: Yes, why not? _____ great!

2 A: _____ on Friday night?
   B: _____, I'm not. I'm going to a concert with Jim on Friday.
   A: Okay, no problem. _____ Saturday instead?
   B: _____ idea. Thanks.

3 A: _____ at 7 p.m?
   B: _____ a swimming class until 7.15.
   A: _____ come along at 7.30? We'll get the tickets and wait for you.
   B: _____ . I'll see you at 7.30 then.

6 the rules

* easy to do
** a bit harder
*** extra challenge

Vocabulary

Brat camp

1 Underline the correct verbs.

1 *get/go* on with someone
2 *make/have* an argument
3 *not take/not get* any notice
4 *get/go* into trouble
5 *go/have* wrong
6 *do/go* badly at school

2 Match 1–6 with a–f to make complete sentences.

1 People go
2 Last year I got
3 I have a good relationship with my parents. I get
4 I gave him some advice, but he didn't take
5 Mike did
6 I never have

a on with them very well.
b wrong in life for many different reasons.
c any notice.
d badly in his exams last year.
e arguments with my sister.
f into trouble with the police.

3 Complete the text with the words below.

> doing badly   wrong   into trouble
> get on with ✓   take any notice of   arguments

Getting help

When Kate moved schools last year she had a lot of problems. She didn't ¹*get on with* her new teachers and she got ² _____ because she didn't do her homework. When her teachers complained, she didn't ³ _____ them. In fact, she had ⁴ _____ with most of them. She started ⁵ _____ at school and she didn't pass all her exams. Finally, her teachers talked to her parents. They found out that Kate was unhappy because she didn't have any new friends. She felt very lonely. Her teachers talked to the other students. Now Kate has lots of friends and she's doing well. Now she talks to other students who go ⁶ _____ to help them solve their problems.

Grammar

Permission in the present

4 (*) Look at the notice on Dominic's bedroom door. Complete the rules with *can/can't*.

> **Dominic's bedroom**
> If you come into my bedroom, follow these rules!
> **No!**
> Don't go in when I'm at school.
> Don't switch off my computer.
> Never borrow my things.
> Don't use my CD player.
> Never read my diary.
> **Yes!**
> Clean my room.
> Bring me snacks.
> Make my bed.
> Help me with my homework.

1 Nobody *can* read Dominic's diary.
2 Visitors _____ switch off Dominic's computer.
3 Visitors _____ take away dirty plates and cups.
4 Dominic's parents _____ go into his bedroom when he is at school.
5 Mum and Dad _____ make his bed.
6 Mum and Dad _____ bring him a sandwich.
7 Dominic's sister _____ listen to music on his CD player.

5 (**) Complete the sentences with the correct form of *be allowed to*.

1 You *are not allowed to* smoke here.

2 You _____ cycle here.

3 You _____ walk on the grass.

4 You _____ swim here.

5 You _____ use a phone here.

6 You _____ have a picnic here.

Obligation in the present

6 ⁂ Liz is on an exchange trip and is staying in a youth hostel with her classmates. Complete the rules with *have to* or *don't have to*.

> **RULES FOR VISITORS:** make beds, keep rooms tidy, cook own food at weekends, wash up after cooking, be quiet after 11 p.m.

> **RULES FOR HOSTEL STAFF:** clean bathrooms, wash sheets and towels, make meals during the week.

1 Visitors *have to* make their beds.
2 Visitors _____ cook their own food during the week.
3 Visitors _____ be quiet after 11 p.m.
4 Visitors _____ clean the bathrooms.
5 The hostel staff _____ do the washing-up.
6 The hostel staff _____ do the washing.

Obligation and permission in the present

7 ⁂ Complete Tom's email from a summer camp with *can/can't, have to/don't have to*.

To: mumdad@cmail.com
From: t.holiday2@dmail.com
Subject: Sports Camp

Dear Mum and Dad,

Sports summer camp is great! The days are long, but fun. We ¹ *have to* get up at six every morning. We ² _____ only sleep late at weekends when we ³ _____ get up until seven – can you believe it?! We ⁴ _____ go to bed between 9 p.m and 10.30 p.m, but I usually go to bed early.

There are lots of activities to choose from. Everyone ⁵ _____ go swimming, cycling or walking, but you ⁶ _____ be over sixteen if you want to go climbing.

Saturdays are rest days, we ⁷ _____ do anything we want. Last Saturday I slept all afternoon! Next Saturday I want to go on a trip to the local town, but you ⁸ _____ go without written permission from your parents. Please write to the camp counsellors so I can go.

It's time for tea so I ⁹ _____ go.

Love

Tom

Grammar reference

Obligation and permission in the present

Form

+	I/He/She/It/We/You/They **can** go now.
	I/We/You/They **have to** go now. He/She/It **has to** go now.
	I **am allowed to** go now. He/She/It **is allowed to** go now. We/You/They **are allowed to** go now.
−	I/He/She/It/We/You/They **cannot (can't)** go now.
	I/We/You/They **do not (don't) have to** go now. He/She/It **does not (doesn't) have to** go now.
	I **am not ('m not) allowed to** go now. He/She/It **is not (isn't) allowed to** go now. We/You/They **are not (aren't) allowed to** go now.

Yes/No questions	Short answers
Can I/he/she/it/we/you/they go now?	Yes, I/he/she/it/we/you/they **can**. No, I/he/she/it/we/you/they **can't**.
Do I/we/you/they **have to** go now?	Yes, I/we/you/they **do**. No, I/we/you/they **don't**.
Does he/she/it **have to** go now?	Yes, he/she/it **does**. No, he/she/it **doesn't**.
Am I **allowed to** go now?	Yes, you are. /No, you are not.
Is he/she/it **allowed to** go now?	Yes, he/she/it **is**. No, he/she/it **isn't**.
Are we/you/they **allowed to** go now?	Yes, we/you/they **are**. No, we/you/they **aren't**.

Wh- questions

Who can I invite to my party?
How much money are you allowed to spend?

Use of *can/can't/have to/don't have to*, *be allowed to/ not allowed to*:

• Use *can* + verb to talk about things that are permitted.
You can keep it if you want.

• Use *can't (cannot)* + verb to talk about things that are not permitted.
You can't smoke in restaurants in this country.

• Use *have to* + verb to say that something is necessary.
My grandma has to have an operation next week.

• Use *don't have to* to say that something is not necessary:
Daisy doesn't have to study French this year.

• Use *to be allowed to* + verb to say that something is permitted.
We're allowed to leave school early today.

• Use *to not be allowed to* + verb to say that something is not permitted.
You aren't allowed to take these books home.

Vocabulary

Rules and behaviour

1 Rearrange the letters in brackets to make words to complete the text.

There aren't very many rules in my house, my parents aren't very ¹ _strict_ (trctis) – in fact they're very ² _____ (yase-niggo). They think parents should ³ _____ (diuge) their children to help them make the right decisions and that they shouldn't ⁴ _____ (norolct) them too strictly. They say that you have to be ⁵ _____ (arfi) and ⁶ _____ (nisuhp) your children if they do wrong, but that you can ⁷ _____ (rignb) children up with a lot of ⁸ _____ (eomdref).

make and *do*

2 Complete the table with the expressions below.

> the hoovering ✓   the housework
> phone calls   the beds   a phone call
> nothing   a mess

make	do
	the hoovering

3 Write sentences to describe the picture using *make* and *do*.

_____

_____

_____

_____

Grammar

Obligation and permission in the past

4 ✳ Read the article about Amelia and complete it with the past form of the verbs in brackets.

Life in the 1800s

Amelia was born in England in the 1800s. Life was very different for women in those days. She ¹ _wasn't allowed to_ (is allowed to) go to university. Women ² ___ (can't) go to university until almost 1900. Only women from rich and upper class families ³ ___ (are allowed to) study subjects such as Music, Art or French but they ⁴ ___ (don't have to) work. In fact, many rich women ⁵ ___ (can't) work because they didn't have enough education or training. Women from poor families ⁶ ___ (have to) work in factories and laundries.

In the 1800s, a woman ⁷ ___ (isn't allowed to) keep the money she earned from her work because she ⁸ ___ (have to) give everything to her husband. Rich women like Amelia ⁹ ___ (aren't allowed to) travel alone, someone always ¹⁰ ___ (have to) accompany them. Amelia ¹¹ ___ (can't) go out with her friends or marry who she wanted. She always ¹² ___ (have to) have the permission and approval of her family. She ¹³ ___ (isn't allowed to) be a doctor, lawyer or politician, in fact she ¹⁴ ___ (can't) even vote. Life was very different in the 1800s!

5 ✳✳ Read the text above again. Tick (✓) true or cross (✗) false.

1 ☐ In the 1800s women could go to university.

2 ☐ Women from rich families had to work.

3 ☐ Women from rich families could study music or languages.

4 ☐ Women were allowed to travel alone.

5 ☐ Amelia couldn't marry without the permission of her family.

6 ☐ In the 1800s women could vote.

6 (***) Complete Sandra's blog with *could/ couldn't, had to/didn't have to* or *was/wasn't allowed to*. Sometimes more than one answer is possible.

My first job

In the summer holidays I had a temporary job in an office. I wanted to get some work experience but there were so many rules.

I [1] *wasn't allowed to* do anything very important. I [2] _____ sit at my desk and answer the telephone all day. The first few days were very boring.

I [3] _____ make lots of tea for everyone and do all the little jobs that no one else wanted to do, for example, photocopying. I [4] _____ touch a computer and I [5] _____ talk to the boss when I went to complain. I [6] _____ wear horrible smart clothes too and I [7] _____ wear trousers. I [8] _____ take thirty minutes for lunch when everybody else got forty-five minutes.

After about a week I [9] _____ do more and the job became more interesting. I [10] _____ learn a lot of new things quickly. It was hard as I [11] _____ remember how to do all the new things. In my last two weeks, I [12] _____ do some really interesting things. I'm going to work there next year and it will be fun – and hard work!

Grammar Plus: Infinitive with and without *to*

7 (*) Underline the correct verbs to complete the sentences.

1 I have *to go/go* now, I'm late.
2 You must *to wear/wear* school uniform, it's obligatory.
3 You should *to talk/talk* to your parents about the problem.
4 Kate isn't allowed *to go/go* to parties during the week.
5 I don't have *to get up/get up* early tomorrow.
6 You can't *to leave/leave* your bicycle here.

Grammar reference

Obligation and permission in the past
Form

+	I/He/She/It/We/You/They **could** stay.
	I/He/She/It/We/You/They **had to** stay.
	I/He/She/It **was allowed to** stay. We/You/They **were allowed to** stay.
−	I/He/She/It/We/You/They **could not (couldn't)** stay.
	I/He/She/It/We/You/They **did not (didn't) have to** stay.
	I/He/She/It **was not (wasn't) allowed to** stay. We/You/They **were not (weren't) allowed to** stay.

Yes/No questions	Short answers
Could I/he/she/it we/you/they stay?	Yes, I/he/she/it/we/you/they **could**. No, I/he/she/it/we/you/they **couldn't**.
Did I/we/you/they **have to** stay?	Yes, I/we/you/they **did**. No, I/we/you/they **didn't**.
Was I/he/she/it **allowed to** stay?	Yes, I/he/she/it **was**. No, I/he/she/it **wasn't**.
Were we/you/they **allowed to** stay?	Yes, we/you/they **were**. No, we/you/they **weren't**.

Wh- questions
What subjects could your parents study?
What TV programmes were you allowed to watch when you were young?

Use of *could/couldn't*:
• Use *could* + verb to talk about things that were permitted in the past.
*Children **could play** in the street when I was young.*

• Use *couldn't* + verb to talk about things that were not permitted in the past.
*I **couldn't catch** the train because I didn't have my train pass.*

Use of *had to/didn't have to*:
• Use *had to* + verb to say that something was necessary in the past.
*My dad **had to go** in the army for two years.*

• Use *didn't have to* + verb to say something was not necessary in the past.
*I **didn't have to wait** long for a bus.*

Use of *to be allowed to/not allowed to*:
• Use *was/were allowed to* + verb to say that something was permitted in the past.
*The children **were allowed to stand** at the front.*

• Use *wasn't/weren't allowed to* + verb to say that something was not permitted in the past.
*My sister **wasn't allowed to wear** her new mini skirt.*

Vocabulary

Society and the law

1 Match a verb in column A with a noun in column B.

A		B	
1	steal	**a**	a crime
2	take	**b**	some money
3	commit	**c**	the army
4	join	**d**	to prison
5	go	**e**	a driving test

2 Complete the crossword.

[crossword grid with answers: 1 across starts I; 2 down starts D; cells numbered 1–10]

Across

1 In many countries you have to carry _ID_ with you at all times.
4 Smoking is ___ in many public places in the UK. You're not allowed to smoke.
7 Which politicians are you going to ___ for in the election?
8 Kate wants to ___ the army.
9 In the UK it is ___ to sell alcohol to people under the age of eighteen.
10 When you kill someone it is ___ .

Down

2 In some countries you can get the ___ ___ if you commit a very serious crime.
3 To ___ means to take things without paying for them.
5 When I pass my ___ ___ , I want to buy a car.
6 In your country, do people go to ___ if they don't vote in elections?

Reading

3 Read the title of the text and look at the cartoons. Choose the best option below, then read and check your answer.

1 The text is about how people write new laws.
2 The text is about funny old laws.

4 Match the underlined laws 1–4 in the text with the pictures a–d.

5 Read the text. Tick (✓) true or cross (✗) false.

1 ☐ All countries have laws.
2 ☐ In Scotland, if people ask to use your bathroom, you must agree.
3 ☐ Taxis in the City of London must only carry living people.
4 ☐ You are not allowed to have a bath in winter in one American state.
5 ☐ You can skateboard in police stations in Miami.
6 ☐ You are not allowed to cut your grass on Sunday in Switzerland.

6 Read the text again and answer the questions.

1 Will you go to prison for breaking these old laws?

_____

2 What must students at Trinity College have if they want a glass of wine in an exam?

_____

3 What is the punishment for stealing soap in Arizona?

_____

4 Can women in Michigan cut their hair when they want?

_____

5 Where are you not allowed to speak English?

_____

6 What household task can't you do on Sunday in Switzerland?

_____

It's the law!

Every country in the world has laws. However in some countries, laws still exist from hundreds of years ago when life was very different. These laws are still legal, but they are never used nowadays because they are completely out-of-date. Many people think the government should repeal* these laws. And you certainly won't go to prison if you break any of these laws!

A _____

In Dublin [1] in Ireland, <u>students at Trinity College can ask for a glass of wine at any time during an exam – but they must have a sword!</u> This law is from long ago when only the sons of rich men went to university and they all carried swords. In Scotland, if someone comes to your house and asks to use the toilet, you have to say yes! A strange English law says that it is illegal for taxis in the City of London to carry dead people – their customers must be alive! [2] <u>There is also an English law about sending letters – you must not put a stamp of the King or Queen upside down on the letter!</u>

B _____

C _____

The USA has some funny old laws, too. In Indiana [3] <u>it is illegal to have a bath in winter.</u> If you steal soap in Arizona – you won't get the death penalty, but you must wash yourself with the soap until you finish it. In Michigan, a woman's hair belongs to her husband, so she is not allowed to cut her own hair without his permission. Perhaps the strangest law is from Illinois – it is illegal to speak English!

And here are the laws we think are the strangest! In Miami, Florida, it is illegal to skateboard in a police station. In Switzerland it is illegal to cut the grass on a Sunday, and you cannot do your washing, either. [4] <u>In Colorado (USA) it is illegal to lend your hoover to your neighbour – so you can't do the hoovering if you haven't got your own hoover.</u> It is illegal to eat a traditional Christmas cake (a mince pie) on Christmas day in England! Why did these things become illegal? We just don't know!

D _____

*When you repeal a law it stops being a law (it is not a law any more).

Reading

True/False/No information

1 Read the following paragraph and the sentences. Tick (✓) true or cross (✗) false or write (?) if the text doesn't say.

> Our school has a science lab with lots of modern equipment. Every week we have one science lesson in the lab and one in an ordinary classroom. The lessons in the lab are fun, but there are a lot of health and safety rules. Our teacher gave everybody a sheet with all the rules. We even had to show it to our parents. The teacher says we must always follow the rules because we don't want any accidents.

1 ☐ The student enjoys the lessons in the science lab.

2 ☐ The school sent a sheet with health and safety rules to parents.

3 ☐ The school created the health and safety rules sheet after an accident.

Exam TIP

The false and 'no information' statements often sound similar to something in the text. You have to find the difference.

2 Look at the sentences you marked (✗) and (?) in exercise 1. What are the differences between those statements and the text?

3 Read the health and safety rules. Tick (✓) true, cross (✗) false or write (?) if the text doesn't say. <u>Underline</u> the parts of the text which helped you decide.

1 ☐ Students are only allowed to enter the lab with a teacher.

2 ☐ Students can bring food into the lab but they mustn't eat it there.

3 ☐ Students have to wear safety goggles all the time.

4 ☐ The teacher will punish students who do not listen to instructions.

5 ☐ Some of the chemicals can burn your hands.

6 ☐ When there's an accident, tell the teacher at once.

The Science Lab

Health and safety rules

Welcome to the school science lab. We hope you enjoy your time in the lab and learn a lot. We also want you to be safe, so make sure you always follow these rules.

- Students must not enter the lab without a teacher. Always wait outside.

- Put your bags on the shelf at the back of the room.

- Students are not allowed to bring any food or drink into the lab.

- During experiments students must wear safety goggles.

- Always listen to the teacher's instructions and do only what he/she tells you to do. Take special care with electrical equipment.

- A mess in the lab can be dangerous! Containers with chemicals should be closed when nobody is using them. Always clean up carefully after experiments, according to the teacher's instructions.

- You should report any accidents to the teacher immediately. If you burn your hand, put it under cold water at once, then ask for help.

Listening

Multiple choice

4a ⑦ Listen to the first part of an interview with a music teacher. Answer the first question. Which phrase in the recording helped you choose the correct option? Write it down.

1 Gerald

a teaches children to play the guitar.

b composes songs for his pupils.

c teaches children to sing.

b ⑦ Read the exam tip. Listen again and correct the wrong answers in exercise 4a.

**Exam TIP**

The wrong answer can use similar words to something in the recording, but the meaning is not the same.

5 (8) **Read the questions. Then listen to the rest of the recording and choose the correct answer.**

1 After listening to *The Carnival of the Animals*, children have to
  a draw the different animals.
  b compose their own piece of music.
  c imitate an elephant.

2 The class listen to Louis Armstrong's song
  a and then they sing it themselves.
  b after they sing it themselves.
  c because the teacher likes jazz.

3 The children
  a mustn't stand up during lessons.
  b sometimes damage the instruments.
  c enjoy dancing.

Use of English

Jumbled sentences

Exam TIP

When putting jumbled sentences in order, pay attention to both meaning and grammar, for example: singular/plural, articles before nouns, prepositions and word order in questions.

6 Underline **the two words that can follow the first word in each line.**

1 He *is/are/was/were*
2 an *athlete/volunteer/orange/strawberry*
3 enjoy *read/swimming/swim/reading*
4 have *go/to go/studying/to study*

7 Put the words in the correct order.

1 meal/healthy/a
  a healthy meal

2 me/than/older
  _____

3 do/ live/you/where
  _____?

4 evening/the/in
  _____

8 Put the words in the correct order to make sentences.

1 cinema/evening/go/to/every/you/the/shouldn't
  You shouldn't go to the cinema every evening.

2 tomato/sugar/an/than/a/more/apple/contains
  An _____.

3 important/I/afternoon/an/in/match/have/the
  I _____.

4 eating/arrived/my/while/lunch/were/friend/we
  My _____.

5 mineral/bottle/have/a/water/I/can/of
  Can _____?

6 family/breakfast/usually/what/have/for/does/your
  What _____?

Speaking

Photo description

9 Read the exam task and complete the comparison of the two photos with the words below.

Look at the two photos and compare them.

| while | too | than | on the right |
| on the left | first | both ✓ |

In [1] *both* photos the women are eating. But in the photo [2] _____ , the food is healthier [3] _____ in the other one. I can see a plate of salad and a glass of juice. This kind of food is good for you. In the photo [4] _____ the woman is eating things which are bad for her: a big hamburger and some chips. She is also eating [5] _____ quickly, [6] _____ the woman in the [7] _____ photo is enjoying a slow, relaxed meal. It is a much healthier way of having a meal.

Vocabulary & Grammar

1 <u>Underline</u> the correct words to complete the sentences.

1 We usually have *tea/<u>breakfast</u>/dinner* at 8 a.m.

2 I'm sorry but I don't eat *sausages/cabbage/rice*. I'm a vegetarian.

3 My Maths teacher is very *fair/easy-going/strict*. We have to sit quietly in his lessons.

4 Can you get a *box/loaf/packet* of bread?

5 I *made/had/did* a big argument with my parents yesterday.

6 Have some more *onions/lettuce/grapes*. Fruit is good for you.

7 I like most dairy products, especially *cheese/ pasta/bacon*.

/6

2 Complete the sentences with one word in each gap.

1 The Neapolitan pizza is the Italian national *dish*.

2 Can I have a glass of orange _____ ?

3 I don't _____ on well with my new boss.

4 Sarah _____ on a lot of weight at Christmas. She needs to eat less now.

5 Can I use your mobile? I need to _____ a phone call to my father.

6 Chocolate biscuits _____ a lot of sugar.

7 I have to _____ the ironing.

8 Can I have one more _____ of cheese, please?

/7

3 <u>Underline</u> the correct forms to complete each sentence.

1 When I was in primary school we *must/<u>had to</u>* wear a terrible dark blue school uniform.

2 We *don't have to/shouldn't* get up early tomorrow – it's Saturday!

3 *Were/Did* your grandparents allowed to come home after 11p.m. on Saturday nights?

4 *Must/Should* I talk with our teacher about it or not, what do you think?

5 In this country you *don't have to/aren't allowed to* buy alcohol if you're under twenty-one – it's illegal.

6 You *have to/can* come to my party with your boyfriend if you like.

/5

4 Complete the sentences with a modal verb from box A and a verb from box B.

A [can't   didn't have to   don't have to ✓
shouldn't   could   should   had to   must]

B [join   stop   lose   make ✓   eat
punish   vote   do]

1 Mum, you *don't have to make* sandwiches for me. I'm not hungry.

2 When I was a child, teachers _____ children by hitting them on the hand when they behaved badly. Now it's not permitted.

3 I think you _____ some weight, Peter. You eat unhealthy foods and are unfit.

4 In my country you _____ for a president until you're eighteen.

5 John has a bad heart and smokes twenty cigarettes a day. He _____ smoking immediately.

6 Mum _____ the cooking yesterday. We all went to a restaurant.

7 My grandfather _____ the army in 1939. He was a very young soldier.

8 You _____ so many biscuits. It's not good for you.

/7

5 Read about Jane's eating habits. Complete the gaps in the text with *a, an, the* or Ø (zero article).

By Jane Perkins

Our Eating Habits

Personally, I think [1] *Ø* teenagers don't care about what they eat. Most of us know a little bit about [2] _____ food and what's good for us. But we don't think about it when we have [3] _____ lunch or go out for [4] _____ meal. [5] _____ meal I had yesterday was not very healthy. I went to [6] _____ fast food restaurant and bought two cheeseburgers with chips. So in [7] _____ evening I only had [8] _____ plate of vegetables. And that was probably [9] _____ best thing I ate yesterday. Everybody knows that [10] _____ vegetables are very good for you. In the future I want to be [11] _____ actress so I should be more careful about my diet. Definitely no more fast food!

/5

Reading

6 Read a page from an information booklet for students starting a secondary school. Tick (✓) true or cross (✗) false.

Dear Student

Welcome to St Luke's School. This booklet has some useful information about your new school. Read it carefully.

Times of the School Day
Students should not arrive at school before 8.00 a.m. On most school days the school closes at 5 p.m. Students must leave the site before 4.00 p.m.

Uniform
Students must wear the school uniform. All items of clothing must be clearly marked with the student's name.
- white shirt (boys), blue/white blouse (girls);
- grey suit (boys), grey skirt and navy-blue pullover (girls);
- blue and white tie (boys), ties not necessary (girls);
- dark grey socks (boys), white/navy socks (girls);
- black shoes (no trainers or boots).

Hair must be clean and tidy, not dyed.
Jewellery and make-up are not allowed.

School Lunches
We have a popular cafeteria which serves hot and cold meals. For a good midday meal you need to spend about £1.85. Students who bring their sandwiches/packed lunches can eat them in the dining hall. Students must not leave the school during the lunch hour.

Library
The library is on the 1st floor. It is open Monday to Friday from 8.30 a.m.–1.15 p.m. and 1.25 p.m.–4.00 p.m. for students, teachers and parents.

Absence from School
When a child can't come to school, we ask parents to phone the school on the first day of absence. When the student returns to school, he/she should bring a letter from their parents to explain their absence.

---

1 ☐ Students can't stay at school after 4.00 p.m.
2 ☐ Students must put their name on their clothes.
3 ☐ Girls don't have to wear school ties.
4 ☐ Students are allowed to wear trainers to school.
5 ☐ All students must bring £1.85 to buy a hot or cold meal in the cafeteria.
6 ☐ The school library is open on Saturdays.
7 ☐ Parents can use the school library.
8 ☐ Parents should call the school and then write a letter when their child is ill.

/8

Communication

7 Complete the two dialogues with the phrases and words below.

[would you like to ✓   don't you bring
you free   great idea   shall we
that would be   afraid   can't]

1

Ted: [1] *Would you like to* come to my birthday party, Sue?

Sue: [2] _____ lovely, thank you. When is it?

Ted: At 5 p.m. on Saturday. Why [3] _____ your boyfriend with you?

Sue: That's a [4] _____! Robert loves parties. [5] _____ bring some food or CDs?

Ted: No, thanks. I've got everything.

2

Tom: Are [6] _____ today?

Nick: No, actually I'm very busy. I'm [7] _____ I have to study for my driving test tomorrow. Why?

Tom: I have problems with our History homework. Do you think you could help me?

Nick: I'm sorry, I [8] _____ today. But how about tomorrow instead?

Tom: That's great, thanks a lot.

/7

8 <u>Underline</u> the correct words to complete the sentences.

A: [1] *Usually/Generally*, people in my country don't drink much tea.

B: [2] *Really?/Yes?* It's completely [3] *similar/different* in my country. Everybody drinks several cups a day. [4] *Personally/Generally*, I love it. It's good for you too.

A: I'm not [5] *agree/sure* about that. It makes your teeth brown!

B: Well, I [6] *agree/don't agree* with that. But you can always brush your teeth after drinking.

/5

Marks

Vocabulary & Grammar	**/30 marks**
Reading	**/8 marks**
Communication	**/12 marks**
Total:	**/50 marks**

*	easy to do
**	a bit harder
***	extra challenge

Vocabulary

Holidays

1 Complete the table with the words below. Which two activities can you do indoors or outdoors?

> camping ✓ shopping swimming
> galleries going to the beach walking
> sightseeing museums sunbathing
> going to clubs looking at scenery

Indoor activities/ places	Outdoor activities/ places
	camping

2 Complete the descriptions with the words below.

> walking excursions nightlife ✓
> relax visit swimming eating
> clubs hanging out

'I like holidays in big cities with lots of
¹ _nightlife_ because I love going to ² _____.
During the day I like ³ _____ with my friends.'
Josh, 15, Cambridge

'When I'm on holiday I don't want to do anything.
I don't want to ⁴ _____ museums or galleries
or go on ⁵ _____. I just want to ⁶ _____!'
Melanie, 16, Manchester

'I like to be active on holiday. I enjoy
⁷ _____ in the sea or ⁸ _____. I like
⁹ _____ out with my family at night.'
Kate, 14, Leeds

Grammar

Future arrangements

3 (*) Put the words in the correct order to make sentences about Natasha's arrangements for the weekend.

1 going out/on Friday night/isn't/she

   She isn't going out on Friday night.

2 Susan/meeting/for lunch/on Saturday/she's

   _____

3 after lunch/a present for Katy's birthday/buying/she's

   _____

4 going/to the cinema/with Pete/on Sunday evening/she's

   _____

5 studying/weekend/she/ this/isn't

   _____

4 (**) Complete the dialogue between Rachel (R) and her cousin David (D) about their holidays. Use the correct form of the verbs in brackets.

R: Hi, David. ¹ _Are you coming_ (you/come) on holiday with us again this year?

D: No, I can't. I'm sorry.

R: Oh that's a pity. Who ² _____ (you/go) with this time?

D: I ³ _____ (not have) a holiday this year. I ⁴ _____ (prepare) for my exams. I failed three so I ⁵ _____ (take) them again in August. Where ⁶ _____ (you/ go)?

R: Greece.

D: Sounds fantastic. Have a great time!

Grammar Plus: Prepositions with future time expressions

5 (**) Underline the correct word to complete the sentences.

1 Anna is going to the dentist _in_/on two days' time.

2 Eddie is taking his exams _the next week/next week_.

3 Sylvia and Bill are going to Paris _at/in_ the weekend.

4 Carrie is going to the cinema _tomorrow/on tomorrow_ so she is meeting Ralf _this weekend/ at this weekend_.

5 Sarah is having a party _in/on_ Saturday.

6 I'm meeting Paula _in/at_ two hours. I must go!

6 (✲✲) James, Mark and Kate are going camping next weekend. Read their conversation and then complete it with the correct form of the verbs below.

> stay   cook   prepare   buy   take x2
> meet ✓   cycle   not go

James: So what time ¹ _are we meeting?_

Mark: 7 a.m. at the station.

James: At the train station?

Mark: Yeah … we ² _____ by bus now because we ³ _____ our bikes. It's easier on the train with bikes.

James: Why do we need bikes?

Kate: We ⁴ _____ to the campsite. James, don't forget, you ⁵ _____ at my house on Friday night.

James: Yes, I know!

Kate: Mark, you don't have to take any food with you. Mum ⁶ _____ some packed lunches for all of us.

Mark: Who ⁷ _____ the map? And the tent?

James: I've got the map and the tent. Don't worry!

Kate: Who ⁸ _____ dinner on Saturday?

Mark: Me. I ⁹ _____ all the food at the supermarket this afternoon.

James: Okay, Kate, I'll see you tomorrow. Mark see you on Saturday.

Mark: Okay, bye.

7 (✲✲✲) Write sentences about your arrangements for the next few weeks. Use the verbs below or your own ideas.

> study   go shopping   go to a nightclub ✓
> play tennis/football/basketball   go camping
> hang out with friends   go sightseeing
> go swimming   go to a party   visit relatives
> organise a party   go to the cinema

1 _I'm going to a nightclub on Saturday evening._

2 _____

3 _____

4 _____

5 _____

6 _____

Grammar reference

Future arrangements

Form

+	I	am ('m) meeting	Jo tonight.
	We/You/They	are ('re) meeting	
	He/She/It	is ('s) meeting	
–	I	am not ('m not) meeting	Jo tonight.
	We/You/They	are not ('re not) meeting	
	He/She/It	is not ('s not) meeting	
?	Am I	meeting	Jo tonight?
	Are we/you/they		
	Is he/she/it		

Short answers

Yes, I **am**. / No, I'm **not**.
Yes, we/you/they **are**. / No, we/you/they **aren't**.
Yes, he/she/it **is**. / No, he/she/it **isn't**.

Wh- questions

When are you meeting Jo?
Where are you meeting her?

Use of the present continuous for future arrangements

Use the present continuous to describe definite arrangements in the future.

They**'re moving** house **next month**.
Are you **going** out **tonight**?
We**'re not having** a holiday **next summer**.

> **Notice!**
> We often give a time phrase to show that the arrangement is in the future.

Time expressions

tomorrow, tonight, this afternoon/winter/year, at the weekend, on Sunday/Wednesday, after breakfast, next Tuesday/week/month, in the next few weeks

Vocabulary

Flying

1 Complete the sentences with the words below.

> destination   departures board
> hand luggage   duty-free shop
> check-in desk ✓   luggage   took off
> boarding card   landed   arrivals gate
> collected his luggage   security
> got off   boarded   passport control

Jed's journey

Jed arrived at the airport and found the
¹ *check-in desk* for his airline. He
checked in his ² _____ and when he
got his ³ _____ he went through
⁴ _____. He had to open his
⁵ _____ when he went through
⁶ _____ because he had some
water in his bag. The ⁷ _____
showed that his flight was delayed so he
bought a few things in the ⁸ _____
Finally, he ⁹ _____ the plane. The
plane ¹⁰ _____ and three hours later
the plane ¹¹ _____ at its
¹² _____ and Jed ¹³ _____
the plane. He was tired when he
¹⁴ _____ and he didn't notice he took
the wrong case. He was going through
the ¹⁵ _____ when a woman
stopped him. She explained he had her
case. It turned out they were both staying
at the same hotel. That
was three years ago –
and they are getting
married next month!

Grammar

may, might and *will*

2 (✳) Match each sentence with the correct description.

1 Foreign travel will be easier for more people in the future.
2 People won't stay at home for holidays.
3 People may live and work in different countries.
a The speaker thinks that it is possible in the future.
b The speaker thinks that it is sure to happen.
c The speaker thinks that it is sure *not* to happen.

3 (✳) Use *will, won't* or *might* to complete the predictions.

1 People *will* have more possibilities to travel in the future, I'm sure.
2 It's really sunny. It _____ rain later this afternoon.
3 Global warming _____ disappear in the future. It's just not possible.
4 We've got a great team. I'm sure my country _____ win lots of medals in the next Olympic Games.
5 I _____ go on holiday with my friends next summer, but I'm not sure.
6 People _____ go on holiday to the moon in the future. It's possible.

4 (✳✳) Read the conversation between Kay (K) who is a teacher, and an interviewer (I) about her predictions for studying in the future. Then complete the text with the correct form of the verbs below.

> not have to learn   use ✓   have
> be able to communicate   be   disappear
> be able to take part   not have to go

I: So how will teaching change?
K: Well, students ¹ *will use* electronic books. I think paper books ² _____ . E-books will be on computers.
I: So, students will use computers much more?
K: That's right. Students ³ _____ to school, they ⁴ _____ in lessons at home.
I: And do you think school subjects will change?
K: Let's see … students ⁵ _____ foreign languages because they ⁶ _____ electronic translators.
I: I agree. People all over the world ⁷ _____ with each other without learning languages.
K: Yes, and finally I think there ⁸ _____ new subjects to study. For example, new technologies.
I: Okay, thank you, Kay.

5 (**) Complete the text with the words below.

> might   will definitely ✓   will   won't x2
> will be able to x2   will have to

Trains of the future?

The maglev train is the fastest train in the world. Its name comes from 'magnet' and 'levitate' – levitate means 'go up in the air'. The train levitates in the air and magnetic energy pushes and pulls it to make it 'fly' over the ground.

At the moment there are no maglev trains in the UK, but this [1] _will definitely_ change in the future. British trains are slow, noisy and they are not good for the environment. Experts say that maglev trains would be good because they don't have engines so they [2] ____ produce any noise. Also, they [3] ____ cause any air pollution because the trains don't use fuel.

There are already maglev trains in Japan that travel around 400 kilometres per hour. Scientists say that soon these maglev trains [4] ____ travel at 580 kilometres per hour. In the future, it's possible that maglev trains [5] ___ reach as much as 4,000 kilometres per hour so passengers [6] ____ travel to different destinations very quickly. One problem is that maglev trains are very expensive to build so people [7] ____ pay more for tickets. Companies are talking about building a transatlantic tunnel so in the future people [8] ___ travel from Europe to the USA in just a few hours.

6 (***) Make your own predictions about these things. Use *will/won't* and *definitely/probably*.

1 people/live on other planets

   People will probably live on other
   planets.

2 planes/travel faster

   _____

3 more people/work at home

   _____

4 global warming/become worse

   _____

5 I/get married in the next five years

   _____

Grammar reference

may, might and *will*

Form

+	I/We/You/They/He/She/It	*will* ('*ll*) *travel* *may/might travel*	*more.*
−	I/We/You/They/He/She/It	*will not* (*won't*) *travel* *may/might not travel*	*more.*
?	*Will* I/we/you/they/he/she/it	*travel*	*more?*

Short answers

Yes, I/we/you/they/he/she/it **will.**
No, I/we/you/they/he/she/it **won't.**

Wh- questions

When will they give me the money back?
What time will you be able to pick me up?

Use of *will/won't*:

• Use *will* + verb if we think something is sure to happen.
Spain will be really hot in August.

• Use *won't* + verb if we think something is sure not to happen.
Our team won't win this year.

The future form of *can* is *will/won't be able to* + verb.
*I'll/**won't be able to tell** you tomorrow.*

The future form of *must/have to* is *will have to* + verb.
*I'll **have to invite** Sam to the party.*

Will + *definitely* or *probably*:

• Use *will* + *definitely/probably* to show how sure we feel.
definitely = very sure
*I'll **definitely phone** you tonight.*

probably = quite sure
*I **probably won't** come.*

Notice the different word order in affirmative and negative sentences:
*I'll **definitely phone** you tonight.*
*I **probably won't phone** you tonight.*

Use of *may/might*:

• Use *may/might* + verb if we think something is possible in the future.
*The traffic **might be** bad tomorrow.*
*Ellen **may come** out with us tonight.*

> **Notice!**
> We don't usually form questions with *may/ might* to talk about the future.

Vocabulary

Describing holidays

1 Read Beth's email to her friend about her holiday. Complete the text with the words below.

> traffic jams   exciting   visited
> delayed   delicious food   relax
> accommodation   lots of fun ✓
> sunburnt   food poisoning

To: Julia.green@c2mail.com
From: Beth.friedley@3dmail.com
Subject: Holiday in Italy

Hi there Julia,

How are you? I just got back from the best holiday ever! I went to Venice in Italy with my aunt and uncle and my two cousins. We had ¹ *lots of fun* . Venice is the most ² _____ city in the world, I think. We ³ _____ so many interesting places. Our ⁴ _____ was great, it was a little hotel on one of the canals. There are no cars in the city. Everyone travels on foot or by special boats called gondolas – and there are no ⁵ _____ ! Some days we just sat in St Mark's Square. It's a great place to have a coffee and ⁶ _____ . The weather was great and I am a little ⁷ _____ . The food was wonderful! I think it's the most ⁸ _____ in the world. Melanie, my cousin, tried all the food. One day we thought she had ⁹ _____ but it was just too many ice-creams and pizza! On the way home the flight was ¹⁰ _____ for three hours but I didn't mind. I met a fantastic Italian guy called Paolo at the airport and we are going to keep in touch. How was your holiday?

Love

Beth

Reading

2 Look at the adverts quickly and choose the best answer.

1 The texts are all

a announcements.   b adverts.   c invitations.

3 Read the adverts again and match four of the sentences below to the gaps a–d in the texts. There is one extra sentence.

1 This is the perfect holiday accommodation for all the family.

2 There are hot showers and a big barbecue area.

3 Do you worry about lost luggage or delayed flights?

4 You can book online or by phone – see below for details.

5 There are many interesting places to visit in the area.

4 Read the texts again and answer the questions.

1 How much is the cheapest flight to Europe?

_____

2 Where can you find more information about flights?

_____

3 Which three places can you go to in the centre of town near the Seaview Hotel?

_____

4 Can you eat out near the hotel?

_____

5 What do you do on the Windsor Castle excursion?

_____

6 How many days is the excursion to Alton Towers?

_____

7 How long does it take to get from the campsite to Edinburgh by car?

_____

8 What is there for children at the campsite?

_____

A

TOP FLIGHTS

Do you hate waiting at the check-in for your flight? a ___

With TOP FLIGHTS you definitely won't arrive late at your destination! We'll look after your luggage, we have never lost anyone's luggage. You can even check in online, so you won't have to wait at the airport!

We are a small airline with small prices – but we can guarantee that your flight will leave on time. We will give you back your money – yes, all your money – for a flight delay of more than thirty minutes!

Flights to Europe from an amazing £39!

Check out our website for details:

www.topflights21.com

SEAVIEW HOTEL

Top hotel only minutes from the beach with wonderful views of the sea. **b** _____ . And it's only ten minutes walk to the centre of town with two museums, a gallery and lots of shops. The town has something for everyone! The nightlife is fun – there are plenty of restaurants for all the family and three fantastic nightclubs.

Single rooms from £65 per night.

Double rooms from £95.

www.seaview12hotel.com

GREEN TOURS

We offer exciting excursions every day! Why not try one of these two great offers? **c** _____ .

1 Windsor Castle – Just £15!!

Excursion includes

visit to the castle

lunch in a local restaurant

shopping in Windsor town

2 Alton Towers Theme Park

Excursion includes

travel to and from the park by bus

park entrance fee

1 night in hotel + evening meal

Adults: £105

Children: £60

For booking details and information go to our website: www.21greentours1.com or phone 0208 542760

RED SQUIRREL CAMPSITE

A beautiful campsite with the best scenery in Scotland! An ideal place if you like camping and walking, but it's great for sightseeing too – Edinburgh is only a one-hour drive.

d _____ . Also, there's a games room for children – but you won't need it because the weather won't be awful!

Small tents £6 per night.
Large tents £10 per night.
Cars £3 per night.

Tel: 01142 3645258 for more information and reservations.

Listening

5 ⑨ Listen to a dialogue between Jackie and Alex about their holidays. Complete the sentences with the correct name, Jackie or Alex.

1 _____ 's flight was delayed.

2 _____ likes shopping.

3 _____ got sunburnt.

4 _____ slept well on holiday.

5 _____ 's sister was ill.

6 _____ had a problem with mosquitoes.

6 ⑨ Listen to the dialogue again. Choose the correct answers.

1 When Alex arrived at his destination, he had
a no clothes. b no books. c no hand luggage.

2 What does Alex say about the weather?
a It was sunny all the time.
b It rained all the time.
c It was only sunny for the second week.

3 In the town near Alex's hotel there were
a some museums. b two nightclubs.
c a lot of places to eat.

4 What does Jackie say about her journey?
a They had to wait a long time at the airport.
b They went to their destination by car.
c The journey was fun, it wasn't boring.

5 In the evening Jackie
a went to bed early.
b sang songs with everyone.
c talked to her new friends.

Writing

A personal letter

1 Read Mark's letter. In which paragraph does he

1. [1] apologise for not writing before?
2. [ ] ask for some news?
3. [ ] describe a social event?
4. [ ] ask how the person is?
5. [ ] describe a recent family event?

2 Match the boxes 1–8 with the parts of the letter a–h.

1. [g] Sign off with an informal expression:
   Lots of love,
   All the best,
   All my love,
   Take care,
   See you soon,
   Love,
   Give my love to

2. [ ] Write your address and the date at the top right-hand side. You can write the date as
   5 May 2010 or 5/6/2010.

3. [ ] Ask for someone's news:
   I'd love to hear all your news.
   Write soon and tell me your news.
   So that's my news.
   What about you?
   What's your news?

4. [ ] Start the letter with *Dear* + the person's name:
   Dear Sue,
   Dear Uncle Ben,
   Don't forget the comma (,) after the name.

5. [ ] Close the letter with an expression such as:
   Well, I think that's everything.
   I hope all is well with you.
   I've got to go now (because).

6. [ ] Write your name after signing off.

7. [ ] Apologise for not writing:
   Sorry I haven't been in touch, but …,
   Apologies for not writing sooner, but… ,
   Sorry I didn't write before but …,

8. [ ] Ask how the person is:
   How are you doing?
   I hope you're well.
   How are things with you?

3 Read Mark's letter again and <u>underline</u> the correct words in the statements below.

1. The writer *uses/doesn't use* short forms.
2. The writer *uses/doesn't use* exclamation marks (!) and underlining for emphasis.
3. The writer *includes/doesn't include* Chris's address.
4. The writer *starts/doesn't start* a new paragraph for a new *idea/topic*.

---

^a 37 Mill Street,
Manchester
MR2 6JB
25 June 2010

^b Dear Chris,

1
^c How are you? I hope you're fine and your exams went well. ^d Sorry I didn't write before, but I am really busy! We had exams last week, and it's an important year for me so that's why I didn't write before. I can't wait for the holidays!

2
We're having our after exams party tomorrow, and I'm sure it will be fun. Everyone from my class is coming and we're all taking some food and drink. We're all going to wear fancy dress, even the teachers! I'm going as Charlie Chaplin – I've got a great costume!

3
Last weekend we had a wonderful family party for my grandmother because it was her 60th birthday. All my cousins and aunts and uncles came, and my brother came back from university. We had big cake and we sang and danced too.

4
^e Well, I think that's all the news. ^f Write soon and tell me your news!

^g Love,

^h Mark

4 Match the sentences to the correct topic a, b or c.

  a describing an event and/or meeting someone
  b describing someone's appearance
  c describing someone's character

  1 [c] She's got lots of friends, because she's popular.
  2 [ ] I went to my friend's eighteenth birthday party, and it was great fun.
  3 [ ] She's quite tall and she's got blond hair and blue eyes.
  4 [ ] We stayed up really late.
  5 [ ] She's very friendly.
  6 [ ] And the best thing is, she likes sports, like me!
  7 [ ] I enjoyed/didn't enjoy the party.
  8 [ ] Guess what? I met a fantastic girl there!!
  9 [ ] She wears casual clothes.

5 Complete the strategies box with the words below.

  [new   right ✓   short forms   short]

A personal letter

- Include your address and the date.
- Start the letter *Dear* …, and sign off with the [1] *right* expression and your name.
- Start with a [2] ___ introduction – greet the person and ask how he/she is.
- Start a [3] ___ paragraph for each separate topic/idea in the letter.
- Finish with the correct expression and ask for his/her news.
- Check your punctuation – did you use: commas (,), apostrophes ('), question marks (?) and exclamation marks (!) correctly?
- Check your style – did you use [4] ___ (*I'm, We're*) and underlining correctly?

6 Read the task and then write your letter. Use the strategies in exercise 5 to help you.

Write a letter to your friend in the USA. In your letter:
- ask how he/she is and apologise for not writing before,
- describe an event and meeting someone new,
- describe his/her appearance and character,
- ask your friend about his/her news and ask him/her to write back soon.

Speaking

Asking for and giving advice

7 Complete the questions with the words below. Then match the questions with the answers.

  [way   best ✓   book   should   recommend]

  1 What's the *best* way to do it?
  2 Where _____ we stay?
  3 Can you _____ any places to visit?
  4 What's the best _____ to get to Oxford?
  5 Do you think we should _____ the hotel?

  a You should definitely stay at the Apple Tree Hotel.
  b Yes, it's always busy. You should phone and book.
  c I don't think you should go to Oxford by bus. Take the train.
  d Don't take the train from Paris. You should fly to London.
  e You must go to Buckingham Palace.

8 Rob is going on a short trip to New York. Marcia was there last year. Complete the dialogue using the phrases below.

  [don't think you should   best to
  you should stay there   should I stay ✓
  must visit   you think I should book
  go by subway   you recommend anything]

Rob: Where [1] *should I stay*, Marcia?

Marcia: Well, I was in a great little hotel near Times Square. I think [2] _____ .

Rob: Okay. Do [3] _____?

Marcia: Yes, I do. It was really busy when I was there so it's best to book in advance.

Rob: Great. Also, I want to see as many things as I can. Can [4] _____?

Marcia: Sure. Well, you [5] _____ the Empire State Building and the Statue of Liberty. They're amazing. The Metropolitan Museum is fantastic too, but it's very big, so it's [6] _____ take a guided tour.

Rob: What about getting around the city?

Marcia: Well, the streets are really busy so [7] _____ if you can. It's much quicker. The New York taxis are famous, but I [8] _____ take a taxi. They're too expensive!

Rob: Thanks for all that advice Marcia!

Marcia: Have a great time!

just do it!

*	easy to do
**	a bit harder
***	extra challenge

Vocabulary

Sports

1 Write in the missing letters to complete the names of sports.

1 f o o t b a l l
2 c r _ ck _ t
3 c y _ l _ n g
4 h o _ k _ y
5 v o l _ e y b a _ _

6 t a b _ e t e _ _ i s
7 b a _ e b _ _ l
8 g _ _ f
9 b a _ _ e t _ a l l
10 t _ n _ i s

2 Which sports from exercise 1 can you see in the picture?

football,

3 Complete the sentences using the words below.

[baseball   cricket   cycling   football ✓
hockey   volleyball]

1 The World Cup is every four years in _football_.
2 There are eleven players on each team in _____ . Everyone wears white. It is very popular in England.
3 _____ has two teams of six players. You can play it on the beach.
4 One of the most important sports in the USA is _____ . The New York Yankees are a famous team.
5 _____ can be dangerous. You usually play in winter. It is very popular in many countries.
6 The Tour de France is one of the most important competitions in _____ .

Grammar

Present perfect with *ever* and *never*

4 (*) Write the verbs in the correct column. Then write the past participle.

[visit ✓ run ✓ travel play try meet
do win watch ride break see
score climb]

Regular	Irregular
visit – visited	run – run

5 (**) Use the prompts to make questions in the present perfect. Then answer the questions.

1 you/score/a goal
   Have you ever scored a goal?
   Yes, I have. / No, I haven't.
2 you/win/a race
   _____
   _____
3 you/try/windsurfing
   _____
   _____
4 you/meet/your/favourite sports personality
   _____
   _____
5 you/climb/a very high mountain
   _____
   _____

6 (**) Look at the list of Julian's experiences and write sentences in the present perfect.

live in France ✗   try surfing ✓
visit Scotland ✓   do yoga ✓
ride a horse ✗   play baseball ✗

1 _He's never lived in France._
2 _____
3 _____
4 _____
5 _____
6 _____

Present perfect or past simple?

7 (✱✱) **Choose the best word a or b to complete the sentences.**

1 They first … two years ago in Madrid.
   a met ✓   **b** have met

2 I … cricket, but I would like to try.
   a never played   **b** have never played

3 … any good books about sports personalities?
   a Did you read   **b** Have you read

4 What … last weekend?
   a did you do   **b** have you done

5 Pete … basketball before, but he's going to have lessons.
   a didn't play   **b** hasn't played

8 (✱✱) **Complete the text with the past simple or the present perfect of the verbs in brackets.**

Snowboarding

When [1] *did snowboarding become* (snowboarding/become) a real sport? It is difficult to say who [2] _____ (invent) the sport of snowboarding, although most people agree that it [3] _____ (develop) because surfers wanted to 'surf' in the snow. People [4] _____ (use) lots of different things as snowboards. In 1965 a company [5] _____ (design) the 'Snurfer' as a child's toy. In 1977 you [6] _____ (can) buy the 'Flying Yellow Banana' which was a bit like a skateboard. Many people [7] _____ (try) to make the sport more official. In 1985 the first snowboarding magazine [8] _____ (start) and it was very popular. More online magazines [9] _____ (appear) in the last few years. Snowboarders [10] _____ (have) a bad boy image in the beginning but that [11] _____ (change) now. Snowboarding is now an Olympic event and the number of snowboarders [12] _____ (grown) to about five million.

Grammar Plus: *been* vs *gone*

9 (✱✱✱) **Put the verbs in brackets into the correct form of the present perfect.**

1 A: *Have you ever been* (you/ever/go) to France?
   B: No, but my brother's there now. He _____ (be) there for three weeks.

2 A: Where _____ (John/go)? He was here a minute ago.
   B: I think he _____ (go) to the sports centre.

3 We haven't got any cheese because I _____ (not go) to the supermarket.

4 A: _____ (Kate/ever/go) to the USA?
   B: No, but her sister _____ (go) twice.

Grammar reference

Present perfect with *ever* and *never*

Form

+	I/We/You/They He/She/It	**have ('ve) met** **has ('s) met.**	the president.
–	I/We/You/They He/She/It	**have not (haven't) met** **has not (hasn't) met**	the president.
?	**Have** I/we/you/they **Has** he/she/it	**met**	the president?

Short answers

Yes, I/we/you/they **have**. / No, I/we/you/they **haven't**.
Yes, he/she/it **has**. / No, he/she/it **hasn't**.

Wh- questions

How many questions has he answered?
Why have you eaten all my sweets?

We form the present perfect with *have/has* + past participle.
Regular past participles are formed with verb + *ed*.
visit → visited   play → played
***Have** you ever **played** badminton?*

Irregular past participles are all different.
*meet → **met**   put → **put***

Use of the present perfect

Use the present perfect to describe actions that happened in the past but are still important now. We do not say when the actions happened.
*John's **broken** his arm so he can't play in the match.* (= it is important because of the match, it isn't important when John broke his arm)

We often use *ever* and *never* to talk about past experiences with the present perfect.

Ever means *at some time in the past but we don't know when*. We only use it in questions.
***Have** you **ever read** any Shakespeare?*

Never means *at no time*. We don't use it in questions.
*My sister **has never been** abroad.*

> **Notice!**
> *go* has two past participle forms – *been* and *gone*. We use *been* to say someone went to a place but is not there now.
> We use *gone* to say someone is on their way to a place or is there at the moment.
> *John has been to France.* (= John has visited France but he is not there now.)
> *John has gone to France.* (= John is on his way to France OR John is in France now.)

Vocabulary

Sports equipment

1 Label the pictures with the words below.

> net ✓   shorts   ball   player   opponent
> ice rink   gloves   skates   stick

1
2
3
4

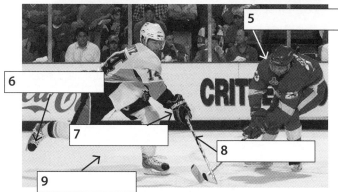

5
6
7
8
9

2 Put the letters in the correct order to make words to complete the sentences.

1 In boxing you wear _gloves_ (velogs) on your hands.

2 Swimmers often use _____ (sloggeg) when they swim under the water.

3 You need a _____ (tiskc) to play hockey.

4 Everyone is so happy when the _____ (croes) is 2–0 for their team.

5 Table tennis is an _____ _____ (donior amge).

6 When a player is tired you send on a _____ (tistubteus).

7 It's great when you _____ (ebat) your opponents, but you don't always have to _____ (niw).

8 You have to _____ (natir) hard if you want to win a _____ (erca).

Grammar

Present perfect with *just*, *already* and *yet*

3 (✱) What has just happened? Write sentences with *just*, the present perfect and the verb in brackets.

1 The bus _has just left_ (leave).

2 Jackie _____ (score) a goal.

3 They _____ (buy) tickets.

4 I _____ (win) the race!

4 (✱✱) Write the dialogue between Sam and his friend, Fred. Use the present perfect and *yet* or *already*.

Fred: Hi, Sam. [1] _Have you bought a camera yet_ (buy/camera)?

Sam: No, [2] _I haven't_ but I bought a map yesterday.

Fred: [3] _____ (look at/the map)?

Sam: Yes, [4] _____. I spent an hour looking at it last night! Hey, [5] _____ (phone/the campsite)?

Fred: No, [6] _____ . Could you do that?

Sam: Yes, sure. And [7] _____ (try out/the tent)?

Fred: Yes, [8] _____ . I slept in it last night! It's fine! And what about food? [9] _____ (buy/the food)?

Sam: No, [10] _____ . I'll buy it tomorrow.

Fred: Okay. Talk to you tomorrow.

Sam: Bye.

5 (✱✱) Sam is going on an adventure holiday next week. Write sentences about what he has already done and hasn't done yet.

> pack his bag ✗
>
> clean his trainers ✓
>
> check the train times ✗
>
> buy new climbing boots ✗
>
> read about the different activities ✗
>
> start a fitness programme ✓

1 *He hasn't packed his bag yet.*

2 _____

3 _____

4 _____

5 _____

6 _____

6 (✱) Underline the correct word to complete the sentences.

1 Petra hasn't finished her lunch *just/yet/already*.

2 Have you heard the news *just/yet/already*? James has *just/yet/already* won fifty euros in a poetry competition.

3 Rob and Silvia have *just/yet/already* been to France. They went last year.

4 Cal and Beth haven't decided which evening classes they want to do *just/yet/already*.

5 A: Have you joined the new gym *just/yet/already*?

  B: Yes, I've *just/yet/already* become a member.

6 I've *just/yet/already* spoken to Frank on the phone. He hasn't left his house *just/yet/already*.

7 (✱✱✱) Complete Fiona's email to her friend, Barry about a new sports centre with the correct form of the verbs in brackets and *just, yet* or *already*.

To: b.jackson@hotmail22.com
From: f.brown@hotmail23.com
Subject: New sports centre

Hi Barry,

¹ *Have* you *heard* (hear) the news *yet*? A fantastic new sports centre ² ____ ____ ____ (open) here. I ³ ____ ____ ____ (be) there to see it. They've got lots of different activities. I ⁴ ____ _____ (join) a swimming class twice a week and I ⁵ ____ _____ ____ (try) yoga for the first time. I ⁶ ____ _____ (decide) to begin Thai-boxing but the classes ⁷ ____(not start) ____ ____ . I saw Chris when I was there. He's going to teach a karate class every week. He ⁸ ____ ____ ____ (offer) to do judo classes as well, but they ⁹ ____ (not begin) ___ _____ .

Let me know when you ¹⁰ _____ _____ (choose) what you want to do and we can go together.

I have to go now because I ¹¹ ____ _____ (not finish) my homework ____ .

Talk to you soon,

Love Fiona

Grammar reference

Present perfect with *just, already* and *yet*

Just, already and yet
We often use *already, yet* and *just* with the present perfect to show that a past action is important now.

Just
We use *just* to say that something happened a little time before now. It is usually used in affirmative sentences.

I've just seen Katrina.
Luca has just had some good news.

Already
We use *already* to say that something happened before the expected time.

Katie's only four, but she's already learnt to read.
I've already done my homework.

Yet
We use *yet* to say that something didn't happen in the past, but will probably happen in the future. *Yet* is usually used in negative sentences and in questions.

Caroline hasn't started driving lessons yet.
We haven't had dinner yet.
Have you finished your exams yet?
Has Will phoned you yet?

Vocabulary

Champions against the odds

1 Match the words 1–6 with the words a–f to make sentences.

1 Anna was already competing
2 Pete is a talented
3 They won
4 We played in
5 She became the chess
6 You need

a a tennis tournament last week.
b world champion in 1996.
c six medals.
d internationally when she was ten.
e strength and speed to swim well.
f disabled athlete.

2 Complete the text with the words below.

> strength   competitions   champion   medal
> competing   tournament   speed ✓

My favourite sports personality is …

Roger Federer. Federer is a Swiss tennis player. He's very fast and strong and he's famous for his [1] _speed_ and [2] _____ on the tennis court. He started [3] _____ when he was a teenager, and at the age of fourteen he became the junior national [4] _____ in Switzerland. In 2001 he won the Milan indoor tennis [5] _____ when he beat Boutter in the final. Since then he has played in many [6] _____ – and won many of them. In 2008 he won an Olympic gold [7] _____ in the doubles with his partner Stanislas Wawrinka. He was the world's number one player from 2004–2008. His tennis heroes are Boris Becker and Stefan Edberg.

Mark, 14, Leeds

Reading

3 Look at the photo and read the first part of the text. Choose the best answer.

1 It is a text about a teenage sports champion.
2 It is a text about teenagers who have become champions.

4 Read the text and answer the questions.

1 How many Olympic medals did Rebecca win in 2008?

_____

2 What do Rebecca's friends call her?

_____

3 What time did training start every morning?

_____

4 Who took Rebecca to training when her sister was in hospital?

_____

5 What did the Queen give her?

_____

5 Read the text again and match sentences a–e to the gaps 1–5 in the text.

a Her mum, Kay, gave up her job to drive her to training.
b She is famous for her speed and strength.
c However, her parents tried to make sure she had a 'normal' life.
d She jumped into a pool on holiday.
e No doubt she will be in the 2012 Olympics too.

6 Read the text again. Tick (✓) true or cross (✗) false.

1 ☐ There was a British Olympic swimming champion in 1988.
2 ☐ Rebecca has loved swimming since she was twelve years old.
3 ☐ Rebecca competed nationally when she was thirteen years old.
4 ☐ Rebecca didn't go out with her friends when she was a teenager.
5 ☐ Rebecca didn't stop training when she was ill.
6 ☐ Rebecca doesn't like chocolate cake.

Champion!

Rebecca Adlington is a British swimming champion. She won two gold medals at the 2008 Olympic Games in the 400 metre and 800 metre races. She is Britain's first Olympic swimming champion since 1988, the first British swimmer to win two gold medals since 1908 – and she is just twenty years old.

Rebecca – or Becky as her family and friends call her – started swimming when she was four years old. [1]_____ 'Oh, no! She's never swum before. Will she be okay?' her mum thought. But Becky swam to the side of the pool, and she's loved swimming since then.

When she was twelve, Becky competed in the national championships and won. Her family realised that she could become a swimming star and Becky started training seriously a year later. [2]_____ Every morning, they drove to the pool very early – training started at 5 a.m. Then they went home for breakfast. Becky went to school just like any other teenager, but after school she went back to the pool for more training. Becky didn't go to parties or nightclubbing as a teenager. [3]_____ Becky's friends often came over to watch DVDs or eat pizza. All Becky's hard work was worth it – she was a member of the British swimming team at the 2008 Olympics. [4]_____

It hasn't always been easy, though. In 2006 Becky's sister Laura was in hospital because she was seriously ill with a disease. Becky also became ill, but not so seriously and she continued training. Her older sister, Chloe, took her to training while the rest of the family was at the hospital. Fortunately, Laura and Becky both recovered completely. The interest from the media – newspapers and TV – has also been a problem. After Becky won her first gold medal, the family spent two days doing TV interviews – from 6.45 a.m. until 10 p.m.!

Becky has already broken many world records and currently holds the record for the 800 metre freestyle race. [5]_____ She also received a special medal, an OBE (Officer of the Order of the British Empire) from the Queen in 2008. The Queen gives OBEs to people who have done work that has helped the country. However, for her family she is still the girl who loves chocolate cake, expensive shoes and watching DVDs!

Reading

Matching short texts

Exam TIP

Make sure the two matched texts agree in all the important details. If one detail is different or missing, the answer is probably wrong.

1 Read about Phil and the kind of holiday he would like to go on. Which words below could you use to describe an ideal holiday for Phil?

> camping   hotel   sightseeing
> action-packed   luxury   activities   city
> sailing   expensive   museum   cheap
> low price   cultural   historic   cycling

Phil is sixteen. He's very active and enjoys all kinds of sports, especially biking and water sports. He'd like to go on a holiday where he could be outdoors and active most of the time, but he knows his parents haven't got much money.

2a Read the holiday descriptions 1–3. Which holiday is the best for Phil? Why?

1 Enjoy an action-packed holiday at our adventure holiday resort for young people. You can try lots of different activities such as sailing, surfing, rock climbing, horse riding and motorbiking. The centre has its own tennis courts and a golf course. Accommodation is in comfortable air-conditioned hotel rooms. Discos every night.

2 Spend an unforgettable week in a stylish hotel in Paris and experience the rich cultural life of France's capital. The price includes guided tours of all the major historic monuments, museum visits, tickets to the theatre and excursions to places of cultural interest in the region. And of course you can go shopping every day!

3 Join our bicycle tour of the beautiful Mazury lakes in Poland. Cycle forty kilometres every morning, go swimming in the afternoon, play volleyball with your new friends if you have the energy left … We are also going to spend one day sailing. Camp in a tent, eat food you cook yourself, and have great fun without spending a lot of money.

b Why are the other two holidays not suitable for Phil? Match reasons a–b to the descriptions.

 a The activities are not what Phil likes doing.

 b The holiday is probably too expensive.

3 Read the descriptions of the people below. <u>Underline</u> the things that are important to each person. Then read holiday advertisements 1–3 from exercise 2a and 4–6 below. Choose the best holiday for each person. There is one extra advertisement.

A ☐ Patricia and Peter are in their thirties. They want to book a holiday for themselves and their baby daughter. They are looking for a relaxing beach holiday with good weather … but they need to keep in touch with their office too.

B ☐ Veronica and Tom are nineteen. On holiday they like to relax on the beach or go swimming during the day, go shopping in the afternoon and party all night in discos and clubs.

C ☐ Luke is fifteen. He's an only child and his parents usually spend a lot of money on his holidays. He likes sports and he'd like to do something different every day. He also enjoys parties.

D ☐ Natalie is a twenty-three-year-old art student. She loves sightseeing and culture. She'd love to see some new places in Europe but she hasn't got much money. She speaks English, French and Spanish.

4 *Would you like to help restore an old castle in Spain?* We need volunteers for this exciting cultural project in the historic region of Catalonia. We offer free accommodation and days off for excursions to historic places such as Barcelona with its great museums, or Reus, home of the great architect Antonio Gaudi.

5 **Have a fantastic holiday on the Mediterranean island of Ibiza,** the clubbing capital of Europe. Sunbathe on the amazing beaches, swim in the blue sea, hang out with friends at the cafés and bars, and dance all night in the best clubs and discos in the world. Non-stop fun guaranteed.

6 **Relax in the Mediterranean sun!** Our comfortable, quiet resort hotel in Alcudia on the coast of Majorca offers perfect conditions for families. Comfortable family rooms with Internet access. Fifty metres from the beach, two swimming pools. Fun activities for children organised every evening.

Use of English

Word formation

4 Complete the table with the words below.

[active   act ✓   actively   activity   actor]

Verb	*act*
Noun (something you do)	
Noun (a person who acts)	
Adjective	
Adverb	

5 Complete the sentences with the words from the table in exercise 4. Sometimes you need a plural form.

1 I like to spend my holidays *actively* .

2 The _____ in the main role was not handsome, but he acted very well.

3 My grandad is sixty-eight, but he's very _____ and does a lot of sports.

4 When I worked as a summer camp counsellor, I organised _____ for children.

6 Write the opposite adjectives. Use the prefixes *in-, il-, ir-, un-*.

happy	*unhappy*
usual	
healthy	
formal	
legal	
regular	

Exam TIP

In word formation exercises, think about the part of speech you need and the meaning. Sometimes you have to form a different part of speech, for example a noun from a verb. Sometimes you have to build a word with the opposite meaning.

7 Complete the text with the correct form of the words in brackets.

When I was younger, I was very ¹_____(fit). If I ever played a sport, it was on the computer! Now I take sports quite ²_____(serious). I jog every morning, swim in the afternoons and I go ³_____(cycle) at weekends. I also enjoy ⁴_____ (danger) activities such as rock climbing and kitesurfing. I think they are ⁵_____ (excite). I even won a local kitesurfing ⁶_____ (compete) last summer. But big ⁷_____ (achieve) are not that important to me. I just enjoy feeling fit and ⁸_____(health).

Speaking

Guided conversation

Exam TIP

Remember to discuss *all* the bullet points in the task.

8 Read the exam task and do the preparation exercises below.

You and your friend are planning a holiday in a city. Discuss and make decisions about:

- ☐ transport
- ☐ accommodation
- ☐ sightseeing/activities
- ☐ things to take
- ☐ problems you might have

a Match sentences 1–5 to the bullet points above in the exam task.

1 You've been there before. Can you recommend any interesting places to see?

2 Do you think we should book a room now?

3 We must take a good map of the city.

4 What if the airline loses our luggage?

5 What's the best way to get there?

b Match responses a–e with sentences 1–5.

a ☐ Yes, and shall we take a guidebook as well?

b ☐ There are some excellent museums and galleries.

c ☐ How about a cheap airline?

d ☐ Yes, we definitely should. Where do we want to stay?

e ☐ Then we'll have to do a lot of shopping!

self-assessment test 4

Vocabulary & Grammar

1 Match the verbs 1–7 with the correct words/expressions a–h.

1 go through   **a** your seatbelt
2 get   **b** the plane
3 visit   **c** food poisoning
4 fasten   **d** your luggage
5 win   **e** your opponent
6 check in   **f** the arrivals gate
7 beat   **g** galleries
8 get off   **h** the race

/7

2 Choose the best word a, b or c to complete the sentences.

1 I love ____ on the beach.
    a sightseeing   **b** sunbathing ✓   **c** camping
2 To play hockey you need a
    a bat.   **b** racket.   **c** stick.
3 What's the best holiday ____ in your country?
    a destination   **b** excursion   **c** journey
4 You can only take five kilogrammes of ____ luggage on the plane.
    a boarding   **b** duty-free   **c** hand
5 You need a ball and a net between the teams to play
    a baseball.   **b** volleyball.   **c** football.
6 Our holiday was great and we ____ lots of fun.
    a had   **b** did   **c** made
7 Look at the departures ____ to see what time our plane takes off.
    a gate   **b** board   **c** card

/6

3 Write sentences in the present perfect using the words in brackets. Use one word/expression from the box below in each sentence.

> passport control   twenty points
> the luggage   four tournaments
> a gold medal ✓   sunburnt

1 (never/ I/win)
    I have never won a gold medal.
2 (ever/you/get/ ?)
    _____
3 (just/we/collect)
    _____

4 (never/Robert/score/in one match)
    _____
5 (already/I/compete in)
    _____
6 (yet/they/go through/?)
    _____

/5

4 Complete the sentences with the correct form of the verbs in brackets. Use the present continuous, *will*, or *might/may*.

1 This summer Gill *'s going* (go) on holiday to Greece.
2 I'm sure Sue _____ (come) late. She's never on time.
3 At the weekend? No problem, I can help you. I _____ (not do) anything important.
4 I don't think I _____ (can) come to your party tomorrow. I need to study for my English test.
5 Laura and Mark _____ (get) married on 17 February. Have they invited you yet?
6 Take an umbrella with you – it _____ (rain). You never know.
7 Don't give Tim sausages. He _____ (not eat) them – he's a vegetarian.
8 The exam was very difficult – I'm not sure but I think I _____ (not pass) it. We will get the results next week.

/7

5 Underline the correct words to complete the sentences.

1 What *will*/<u>*are*</u> you doing on Saturday, Nick?
2 Last week I *have run/ran* four miles.
3 In the future people *definitely will travel/will definitely travel* more by plane.
4 Has Tom ever *drove/driven* a car?
5 Okay, you can watch TV now but you *will/must/have to do* your homework tomorrow after school.
6 The teacher's *yet/already* told us three times about the test on Monday.

/5

Reading

6 Read a page from Jessie's blog and tick (✓) true or cross (✗) false.

18 April

I've tried all sorts of team sports: basketball, volleyball, and even baseball. But football? Everybody thinks it's a boy's sport. When I told my father this morning, he said 'Can't you take up some other sport?' My mother asked, 'Football, Jessie? Are you sure?' I am sure. I want to try for the football team in my new school.

19 April

In the morning Liz and I went to the gym. When we walked through the gym door, the boys turned to look at us. They didn't look pleased to see us. The football coach was really nice and welcomed us.

There are only sixteen places in the school football team. This means half of us will have to do some other sport. A lot of competition! I'm sure Liz will beat some of these boys – she's really fit and has been a substitute for another team. I might not get in the team. But I'll definitely train hard and who knows?

21 April

Yesterday was the first day of practice. We had an 800 metre race and I came ... last. I did my best but the distance was too long for me. Later, we played more football. I tried really hard but I couldn't kick the ball. Then running again. Five times around the school. My feet hurt so I took a long break and sat down on the grass. And the coach was still not happy with some of us. This morning I couldn't get out of bed. I asked myself, 'Do I really want to do it? I might take up tennis instead.'

1 ☐ At first Jessie's parents didn't like her idea.

2 ☐ The boys were very happy when they saw the girls in the gym.

3 ☐ The football coach wasn't friendly, when the girls arrived.

4 ☐ Liz has played football before.

5 ☐ Jessie found it difficult to kick the ball.

6 ☐ Jessie wants to try another team sport.

/6

Listening

7 (10) Listen to the conversation between a travel agent and two customers. Choose the correct answers.

1 The woman and the man have just returned from
   a France.   b Spain.   c Greece.

2 Their plane was delayed by ____ .
   a one hour   b two hours   c three hours

3 Another problem was that
   a the taxi from the airport to the hotel was late.
   b the receptionist at the hotel only spoke some English.
   c the man and the woman didn't get the room they wanted.

4 The woman was unhappy because
   a the holiday was very expensive.
   b she paid for something she didn't get.
   c she didn't like the hotel car park.

5 The travel agent will
   a give the money back to the tourists.
   b call the hotel where the tourists stayed.
   c not talk about the problem with his boss.

6 The man and the woman
   a won't go on holiday with this agency in the future.
   b might go on holiday with this agency again.
   c are going on holiday with this agency next week.

/6

Communication

8 Complete the dialogues with one word in each gap. You can see the first letter of each word.

1 A: We had a horrible time on holiday!
   B: Really? What h_appened_?

2 A: What's the best w_____ to get there?
   B: D_____ fly. Go by train.

3 A: We'd like to do some sightseeing. Can you r_____ anything in London?
   B: You m_____ go to the British Museum.

4 A: H_____ was your holiday?
   B: It was t_____ ! It rained every day.

5 A: Do you think we s_____ stay there?
   B: Yes, d_____ . It's a very good hotel.

/8

Marks

Vocabulary & Grammar	/30 marks
Reading	/6 marks
Listening	/6 marks
Communication	/8 marks
Total:	/50 marks

* easy to do
** a bit harder
*** extra challenge

Vocabulary

Operating machines

1 Complete the sentences with the words below.

> digital camera ✓   console   hairdryer
> flat screen   answering machine
> alarm clock   MP3 player

1 I bought a new *digital camera* to take pictures on holiday.

2 Anna always listens to her _____ when she goes running.

3 I need an _____ to wake me up in the morning.

4 Leave a message on the _____ if Pete's not at home.

5 Alex has got a modern TV – it's a _____ TV.

6 My _____ has broken, so I can't dry my hair.

7 We need a games _____ for this new game.

2 Read the descriptions of gadgets from exercise 1. What are they?

1 You plug it in to the TV and press buttons or use the controls to play.

games console

2 It's got batteries, but it doesn't have a charger. It hasn't got a control button for volume and it's very loud! You have to set the time. I switch it on every night and it helps me wake up!

_____

3 It's got a battery and it has a menu. You don't use a remote control to switch it on and off, you just press a button. Some people have one on their mobile phone, but I don't.

_____

4 It hasn't got any batteries. You plug it in and use a remote control to switch it on and off. You watch things on it. You can select from the menu, but you can't record messages.

_____

Grammar

Relative clauses

3 (*) <u>Underline</u> the correct relative pronoun to complete the sentences.

1 A teacher is someone *which/who/where* helps students to learn about different subjects.

2 A radio is a machine *that/who/where* allows us to listen to different programmes and music.

3 A football stadium is a place *who/which/where* footballers play matches.

4 An encyclopedia is a book *that/who/where* we can find information on almost everything.

5 An actor is a person *that/where/which* appears in films.

6 A school is a place *which/where/who* students go to learn.

4 (*) Read and complete the text about underwater MP3 players with *which, where, that* or *who*.

Underwater music

This is a fantastic gadget for people [1] *who* love swimming and listening to music. The people [2] _____ invented it wanted to give swimmers a gadget [3] _____ allowed them to listen to their favourite songs under water. Now swimmers can listen to music in places [4] _____ it was impossible to listen before, such as in the sea or at the bottom of a pool. In 2007 the company developed a more advanced product [5] _____ makes the music sound even better. It sends special sound waves [6] _____ give very clear sound to the ear. The underwater MP3 player is now used by more than 35,000 people [7] _____ never go swimming without it.

5 (✱✱) **Match phrases 1–6 with phrases a–f. Then add** *who,* *which* **or** *where* **to form complete sentences.**

1 An Internet café is a place *where*

2 A washing machine is a gadget _____

3 A calculator is a machine _____

4 An IT consultant is someone _____

5 A meeting point is a place _____

6 An inventor is a person _____

a likes creating new gadgets.

b people can go to use computers.

c saves time cleaning dirty clothes.

d people usually meet at airports or other big buildings.

e can help you to do Maths.

f solves problems with computer programmes.

6 (✱✱) **Use the prompts to make sentences.**

1 a telescope/piece of scientific equipment/allows us to see the stars clearly.

A telescope is a piece of scientific equipment which allows us to see the stars clearly.

2 a plane/a type of transport/allows us to travel quickly between countries

_____

3 a bicycle/a type of transport/doesn't use any fuel

_____

4 a beach/a place/we go to sunbathe and relax

_____

5 an astronaut/person/travels into space

_____

6 an MP3 player/a gadget/allows us to keep a lot of music in a small space

_____

7 (✱✱✱) **Join the sentences using the correct relative pronoun. Make any necessary changes.**

1 That's the boy. He's in my class at school.

That's the boy who is in my class at school.

2 A scientist is a person. He/She does experiments.

_____

3 A hairdryer is a gadget. It dries wet hair.

_____

4 That's Mr Rad. He's a teacher in my school.

_____

5 A hot spot is a place. People go there to connect their computer to the Internet.

_____

6 A computer mouse is a thing. It lets you move around the computer screen.

_____

Grammar reference

Relative clauses

We use relative clauses to put more information in a sentence. We can join two shorter sentences together, using a relative pronoun.

The Japanese have invented a robot. It can tidy your bedroom.
*The Japanese have invented a robot **which** can tidy your bedroom.*

I've got fifty pounds. My grandmother sent it for my birthday.
*I've got fifty pounds **that** my grandmother sent for my birthday.*

Relative pronouns: *which, that, who, where*

• Use *which* and *that* for things.
*A lawnmower is a machine **which/that** cuts the grass.*
*Adam's got a really expensive phone **which/that** his uncle gave him.*

• Use *who* and *that* for people.
*A babysitter is someone **who/that** looks after kids.*
*That's the boy **who/that** Alice likes very much.*

• Use *where* for places.
*This is the house **where** I grew up.*
*At the weekend, we went to a shop **where** they sell cheap TVs.*

Vocabulary

Gadgets

1 Complete the descriptions with the names of the gadgets.

① My favourite gadget is my _____ . I can listen to my favourite music any time.

② I love my _____ . I spend hours every day on the Internet.

③ The best gadget we have is the _____ . We're all TV addicts, so we use it a lot!

④ Don't laugh, but my favourite machine is my _____ . You can set it to the radio and it's so nice to wake up to music.

2 Complete the sentences with the phrases below.

> easy to carry   go wrong   can't live without
> digital junkies   breaks down ✓

1 I hate it when my computer _breaks down_. I can't email any of my friends.

2 I love my new digital camera. It's really small and _____ ___ _____.

3 My brother _____ _____ _____ his computer games. He plays for hours every day.

4 My father hates all electronic gadgets. He says that we are a generation of _____ _____.

5 When alarm clocks and computers _____ _____ they cause lots and lots of problems.

Grammar

First conditional

3 (✱) Match 1–6 with a–f to form complete sentences.

1 Lisa will miss the train
2 Liam will sing his favourite song
3 If you don't want to go to the club,
4 If Ben and Martin don't go to camp this summer,
5 Martin will tell Ruth about the party
6 If they don't buy the tickets for the concert now,

a they won't see Maggie this year.
b if she doesn't leave soon.
c if he sees her this afternoon.
d there won't be any tickets left.
e if he goes to the karaoke competition.
f you'll have to tell Pete by 6 p.m.

4 (✱✱) Underline the correct words to complete the sentences.

1 If schools _make_ /will make uniforms obligatory, students concentrate/will concentrate more on their lessons and not on their clothes.

2 If you study/will study hard, you pass/will pass the exam.

3 I buy/'ll buy a new iPod if I go/'ll go into town on Saturday.

4 If they don't go/won't go away at the weekend, they go/will go to the cinema on Sunday.

5 What do you do/will you do if John doesn't phone/won't phone?

6 They don't go/won't go for a walk if the weather isn't/won't be good.

5 (✱✱) Put the verbs in brackets into the correct tense.

1 If the restaurant _doesn't have_ (not have) pizza, I_'ll order_ (order) a hamburger.

2 Julia _____ (buy) a new CD if she _____ (go) into town on Saturday.

3 Richard and Matt _____ (not go) to university if they _____ (not pass) their exams.

4 If it _____ (rain) tomorrow, we _____ (not go) on a picnic.

5 _____ (Colin/be) happy if he _____ (win) the race?

6 Isabel _____ (not meet) David this evening if he _____ (not phone) her before 5 p.m.

6 (✲✲✲) **Complete the sentences about yourself.**

1   If the weather is bad this weekend, _I'll watch DVDs all weekend._

2   If I get some money for my next birthday, I

   _____

3   If my best friend isn't happy, I

   _____

4   If it's good weather next week, I

   _____

5   If there isn't anything interesting on TV tonight, I _____

6   If I get a lot of homework this week, I

   _____

7 (✲✲) **Rewrite the sentences with the same meaning using the words in brackets.**

1   I'll finish this exercise, then I'll phone Joanne. (after)

   I'll phone Joanne after I finish this exercise.

2   Sam will have dinner. Then he'll watch his favourite TV programme (before)

   _____ .

3   Mark will finish his homework. Then he'll go out with his friends. (when)

   _____ .

4   Rosa will tidy her bedroom. Then she'll go out to the disco. (after)

   _____ .

5   We'll finish class. Then we will go to the sports centre. (when)

   _____ .

6   I play my computer game but I'll study for another hour first. (before)

   _____ .

Grammar Plus: *if* vs *when*

8 (✲✲) **Complete the sentences with *if* or *when*.**

1   I'll go to the supermarket now. I'll make lunch _when_ I get back from the supermarket.

2   I might see Jackie later. I'll give Jackie your message _____ I see her.

3   We might be tired tonight. We'll go to the sports centre _____ we all feel okay.

4   John is arriving at 11 a.m. I'll phone you _____ John arrives.

5   I'll finish my homework first. I'll watch TV _____ I finish my homework.

6   It's possible they may see Tom at the party. They'll talk to Tom _____ they see him at the party.

Grammar reference

First conditional

We use the first conditional to talk about a possible future situation. But after *if* we use the present tense, not the future.

Form

Condition *If* + present simple	Result *will/won't* + infinitive without *to*
*If I **have** time,* *If you **don't** tell me,* *If Anna **passes** her exams,*	*I **will ('ll) call** you tonight.* *I **will ('ll) be** upset.* *she **will ('ll) start** university in the autumn.*
*If he **doesn't eat** his lunch,*	*he **will not (won't) get** any sweets.*
*If I **help** you with Maths,*	***will** you **help** me with English?*

If can go at the beginning or in the middle of the sentence. When we put the *if* clause first, we use a comma (,) to separate the two clauses.

***If** it's sunny, we'll have a picnic.*
*We'll have a picnic **if** it's sunny.*

Future time clauses with *when, before* and *after*

We also use the present tense to talk about the future after time words like *when, after* and *before*.

*I'll get my sister's bedroom **when** she **leaves** home.*
***Before** I **go**, I'll give you my phone number.*
*Vanessa will probably call **after** I **go** out.*

Vocabulary

Numbers and dates

1 Read the words and write the numbers.

1 nine hundred and seventy-two. *972*

2 nineteen ninety-seven _____

3 eighty-six percent _____

4 three point two million _____

5 a quarter _____

6 seven billion _____

2 Read the amazing facts and write the underlined numbers as words.

Did you know …

1 There are more than 6,000,000 parts in some big aeroplanes.

2 Every year 20,000,000,000 coconuts are grown.

3 People usually read 25% slower from a computer screen than on paper.

4 The Amazon River is more than 6,450 kilometres long.

5 Every letter in the English language is used in the sentence: 'The quick brown fox jumps over the lazy dog.' That means there are 26 in total.

6 The Indian railway system employs more than 1,400,000 people.

1 *six million*   4 _____

2 _____   5 _____

3 _____   6 _____

3 Complete the sentences with the words below.

> search   chat   generation   devices ✓
> background noise

1 We live in a time of electronic *devices*.

2 I like _____ when I'm studying so I often play music.

3 My friends and I _____ on the phone every day.

4 The younger _____ in the UK watches less television than their parents.

5 Vivian loves to _____ for information on the Internet.

Listening

4 ⑪ Check you understand the words below and then listen to the radio interview about *YouTube* and choose the correct answers.

> **an agreement** (n) an arrangement or decision to do something by two or more people
>
> **block access** (v) to stop people being able to enter somewhere (for example a website)
>
> **a founder** (n) a person who starts a company or organisation
>
> **upload** (v) to send documents, photos and videos from your computer to a larger system using the Internet

1 Jawed Karim put the first video on *YouTube* on April … 2005.

   a three   b thirteen   c twenty-three

2 The three people who created the site sold it in 2006 for

   a 6.5 billion dollars

   b 1.65 million dollars

   c 1.65 billion dollars

3 About how many hours of videos are put onto the site every minute?

   a thirteen   b thirty   c fourteen

4 What percentage of people who use online video sites use *YouTube*?

   a 34 percent   b 44 percent   c 54 percent

5 *YouTube* is probably the … most popular video site on the Internet.

   a third   b fourth   c fifth

6 When did *YouTube* make an agreement with three big TV and film companies?

   a 2006   b 2008   c 2010

5 ⑪ Listen again. Tick (✓) true or cross (✗) false.

1 ☐ The first video on *YouTube* showed one of the site creators at the zoo.

2 ☐ There are no age limits on any of the videos.

3 ☐ Alex gives information about the number of videos people watch every year.

4 ☐ If you want to watch a film, you'll have to watch the adverts too.

5 ☐ At the moment there are some countries where you can't watch *YouTube*.

6 ☐ Some schools have blocked access to *YouTube* because students watched videos of bad behaviour.

Reading

6 Look at the photo and title of the text. Read the paragraph headings in exercise 7. Then choose the best answer.

1 The text is about

a different uses of the Internet in the future.

b how teenagers will use the Internet in the future.

7 Read the text and match the headings a–g with the paragraphs 1–6. There is one extra heading.

a Internet and mobile phones

b How will people use the Internet?

c The future of the Internet?

d Other gadgets

e Work and free time

f Science

g How people used the Internet

8 Read the text again and answer the questions.

1 How many websites are there?

_____

2 What will scientists around the world be able to do?

_____

3 What will NASA use their new technology for?

_____

4 Why didn't many people use the Internet on mobiles in 1996?

_____

5 Where can Electrolux fridges send emails?

_____

6 What kind of surface will people be able to display virtual keyboards on?

_____

7 What could people do in gyms in the future?

_____

The Web of the Future

1 _____

When the Internet became generally available in the 1990s nobody had any idea of just how popular it was going to become. There are over a hundred million websites, although nobody knows exactly how many there are, and there are billions of web pages. But what will the Internet be like in the future? Here, the experts give us their predictions.

2 _____

There will be lots of exciting developments in science for using the Internet. For example, scientists around the world will be able to share equipment such as special microscopes called 'electron microscopes'. The American space agency NASA has developed a 'Virtual Collaborative Clinic'. This allows doctors to find out more about diseases and to practise difficult operations in 3D. NASA plans to use the technology to provide health care on long space journeys.

3 _____

The first mobile phone with Internet was in Finland in 1996, but it was very expensive so not many people used it. Japan started the first mobile phone Internet service in 1999. By 2008, more people were using mobiles to access the Internet than computers. In the future, experts say we'll all use our mobiles to access the Internet. Mobile screens will probably get a little bigger, but not much. Of course, you'll control all the functions by pressing the screen, not buttons.

4 _____

Soon, everything from your car to your fridge will be connected to the Internet, and machines will communicate with each other. Electrolux has already developed a fridge that emails a shopping list to a local supermarket – and arranges a time for them to deliver your shopping to your house!

5 _____

We will see a big change in the way people use it. 64 percent of experts think people won't have to use the traditional keyboard. We will have 'virtual' keyboards – people will be able to display these keyboards on any flat surface, such as a table. They will write their email messages using these virtual keyboards and be able to surf the Internet too.

6 _____

Most people will also spend part of their day in virtual worlds, at home or at work. Finally, there won't be a big difference between work and free time. People will be able to connect to the Internet anywhere and work where they are – in the gym, a shop, at home or even in a virtual office.

Writing

A letter of complaint

1 Read the letter and answer the questions.

1 Why is Christine writing?

_____

2 What two problems does she talk about?

_____

3 What does she expect to happen as a result of her letter?

_____

2 Complete the gaps a–f in exercise 1 with the words and phrases below. Read the letter again to help you.

> Secondly, …   Yours sincerely   when
> Dear + name   address ✓
> I look forward to your prompt response.

1 Write your address in the top right corner.

2 Write the date below your **a** _address._

3 Write the name and address of the company you are writing to.

4 Begin the letter *Dear Sir* or *Madam,* or **b** _____, *Dear Mr Stone,*

5 In the first paragraph say why you are writing. Give the details of the product, and say where and **c** _____ you bought it.

6 In the second paragraph explain the problem in detail. Use sequencing words to introduce each separate problem:
Firstly, …
d _____
Thirdly, …
Finally, …
This will help the reader to follow your explanation.

7 In the third paragraph say what you want to happen as a result of your letter.

8 In the fourth paragraph show that you expect a reply:
I look forward to hearing from you as soon as possible.
e _____

9 Close the letter with *Yours faithfully* if you started it with *Dear Sir* or *Madam.*
If you put *Dear* + name, close the letter with **f** _____.

10 Sign the letter.

11 Print your name underneath or write it in CAPITAL LETTERS.

Customer Services,
Everton Electronics,
6 Lonsdale Road,
London SW3 2JM

13 Green Road
London SW1 4BB
15 May 2010

Dear Ms Reid,

I am writing to make a complaint about an ADL W34 flat screen television that I bought from Nixon Stores on 10 May.

There are two problems with the television. Firstly, the remote control does not work properly: sometimes it is impossible to change the channel or turn the volume up. Secondly, when you switch the television on, the picture is not clear for the first five minutes so it is impossible to watch anything until the television warms up. I took the television back to the store, but the manager told me I had to contact you directly.

I am enclosing a copy of the receipt. Could you please send me a new television and pick up the old one or give me a refund as soon as possible?

I look forward to hearing from you.

Yours sincerely,

Christine Brown

Christine Brown

3 Match 1–6 with a–f to form complete sentences. Then say in which paragraph in a letter of complaint you would find the phrase.

1 I am writing to
2 I am returning
3 Could you send me
4 I would be grateful if
5 I am enclosing the CD player
6 I look forward

a you could repair the CD player.
b make a complaint about a CD player.
c to hearing from you in the near future.
d a replacement as soon as possible?
e and the receipt.
f the CD player to you.

Paragraph 1: 1 _b,_ _____

Paragraph 3: _____

Paragraph 4: _____

4 <u>Underline</u> the correct preposition to complete the sentences.

1 I am writing about a fault _with/to/about_ the computer that I bought _with/on/from_ your website.
2 I would like to complain _with/to/about_ the MP3 player which I bought _in/on/off_ your store.
3 I look forward _with/to/about_ hearing _from/to/about_ you.
4 I am sending the printer back _with/to/about_ you _with/to/about_ this letter.
5 When you switch the computer _on/to/in_, the screen stays blank.
6 I have put new batteries _in/on/off_ the phone but it still does not work.

5 Complete the strategies box with the words below.

[explain   detail   date ✓   Secondly,]

Letter of complaint

- Make sure you write the addresses and ¹ _date_ in the correct places.
- Say where and when you bought the product and ² _____ why you are writing in paragraph one.
- Explain the problem(s) in ³ _____ in paragraph two.
- Use sequencing words: _Firstly,_ ⁴ _____ to make your letter easier to follow.
- Remember to say what you want as a result of the letter.

6 Read the task and then write your letter of complaint. Use the strategies in exercise 5 to help you.

You bought a new gadget from a website. You aren't happy with it. Write a letter of complaint.
- Briefly give details about the gadget and when you bought it.
- Complain that you had to wait a long time for it to be delivered and that you didn't receive a reply to your questions for a long time.
- Give at least two reasons why you are unhappy with the product.
- Say what you expect in response to your letter.

Speaking

Complaining

7 Match the problems 1–4 with the expressions for complaining a–d.

1 There is a problem with your new iPod.
2 You want to speak to the person responsible in the shop.
3 You are not satisfied with the situation.
4 You want your money back.

a Could I speak to the manager, please?
b I'd like a refund, please.
c It doesn't work properly.
d I'm really not happy about this.

8 Imagine you are a shop assistant. Write the correct expressions to respond to the situations.

[I'm afraid we can't give refunds.
Have you got the receipt?
What exactly is the problem?
I'm sorry, there's nothing I can do. ✓
We can exchange it if you like.]

1 You can't do anything to help the customer.
I'm sorry, there's nothing I can do.

2 You want the customer to explain what is wrong.
_____ .

3 You want to see when the customer bought the product.
_____ .

4 You can offer the customer a new or similar product to replace the old one.
_____ .

5 You have to tell the customer that you can't give them their money back.
_____ .

10 out there

* easy to do
** a bit harder
*** extra challenge

Vocabulary

The natural world

1 Look at the picture and put the letters in the correct order to make words.

1	trefos	_forest_	5	eas	_____
2	dilef	_____	6	vewas	_____
3	keal	_____	7	adsinl	_____
4	astoc	_____			

2 Read the text about explorer Steve Buck. Then complete it with the words below.

> desert   continent   volcano   rivers
> mountain   the Earth ✓   island   sea
> mountain ranges   Ocean

I'm Steve Buck and I'm an explorer. I've travelled all over ¹ _the Earth_ – it's an amazing planet! I've swum in the Nile and the Amazon, the world's two longest ² _____ and I've swum in the Mediterranean – it's a lovely warm ³ _____ . I've climbed Everest, the highest ⁴ _____ in the world. I've crossed the Sahara, the driest ⁵ _____ in the world. I've travelled by boat across the Atlantic ⁶ _____ – it has really big waves! I've walked over the Alps and the Dolomites, two big ⁷ _____. I've been to see Mount Etna – it's a dangerous ⁸ _____! At the moment my favourite ⁹ _____ is Europe. But when I'm old I want to live on a beautiful ¹⁰ _____ in the Caribbean, like Cuba.

Grammar

used to

3 (*) Complete the sentences with the correct form of *used to* and the verbs in brackets.

1 People _used to think_ (think) that the Earth was flat.

2 _____ (you/believe) in Santa Claus?

3 The Sahara Desert _____ (not/be) sandy, it _____ (be) green.

4 Where _____ (you/spend) your holidays when you were a child?

5 _____ (the River Thames/freeze) when it was very cold?

6 Our grandparents _____ (not/have) CDs or mobile phones.

4 (**) Choose the correct answers. If both answers are possible, choose both.

¹ ___ Britney Spear's life ___ very different when she was younger? Yes! She ² ___ gymnastics when she was a little girl and she ³ ___ in tournaments in Louisiana. She also ⁴ ___ in dance shows and, one night, she ⁵ ___ in her local church. At that time, she ⁶ ___ professionally. She also ⁷ ___ in a Disney programme on TV for two years. She ⁸ ___ her first solo record in 1998 and she's been famous since then.

1 a Was
  (b) Did …. use to be
2 a started
  b used to start
3 a competed
  b used to compete
4 a performed
  b used to perform
5 a sang
  b used to sing
6 a didn't sing
  b didn't use to sing
7 a appeared
  b used to appear
8 a released
  b used to release

5 (*) Rewrite the verbs using *used to/didn't use to*.

Life [1] was/_used to be_ very different two hundred years ago. Most houses [2] didn't have/_____ bathrooms or water inside. There [3] weren't/_____ any radiators to keep the house warm. Winters [4] were/_____ freezing so people [5] wore/_____ lots of clothes. In the evening they [6] sat/_____ around the fire and [7] told/_____ stories because there was no electricity.

6 (**) Read about Brad Pitt. Complete the text with the correct form of the verbs in brackets. Use *used to/didn't use to* where possible. If not, use the past simple.

Brad Pitt

[1] _used to live_ (live) in Oklahoma when he was a child. When he was younger he [2] _____ (dream) about being an actor so he [3] _____ (move) to Los Angeles in 1985. However, he [4] _____ (not succeed) immediately. In the beginning, he [5] _____ (work) for a restaurant and he [6] _____ (have to) wear a big chicken costume to advertise the restaurant! Finally, in 1988 he [7] _____ (get) his first film part, but he [8] _____ (not become) famous until 1991 when he [9] _____ (star) in *Thelma and Louise*.

7 (***) Write sentences using *used to* and *didn't use to* about when you were younger. Use the ideas below to help you or your own ideas.

> love   believe   be frightened of   have
> hate ✓   like   play   listen to   vegetables ✓
> monsters   spiders   favourite toy   computer
> iPod   MP3 player   mobile phone

1 _I used to hate vegetables._
2 _____
3 _____
4 _____
5 _____
6 _____

Grammar reference

used to

Use

• Use *used to* to talk about states in the past that are not true now.

*I **used to be** very shy when I was young.* (= I'm not shy any more)
*We **used to have** a dog.* (= We haven't got a dog now)

• We also use it to talk about things that happened regularly in the past, but have changed now.

*Tom **used to play** football a lot but he stopped when he broke his leg.*
*When I was a child I **used to cycle** everywhere, but now I'm too lazy.*

Form

+	I/He/She/It/We/You/They	*used to* work in the past.
–	I/He/She/It/We/You/They	*didn't use to* work in the past.
?	*Did* I/he/she/it/we/you/they	*use to* work in the past?

Short answers

*Yes, I/he/she/it/we/you/they **did**.*
*No, I/he/she/it/we/you/they **didn't**.*

Wh- questions

Where did he use to go on holiday?
What films did you use to like when you were younger?

> **Notice!**
> We can always use the past simple instead of *used to*.
> *I **used to be** frightened of the dark when I was young.*
> (= I **was** frightened of the dark when I was young.)

There is no present form of *used to*.
Past: *I **used to ride** a lot.*
Present: *I **ride** a lot.*

Vocabulary

Global warming

1 Match the words 1–5 with the definitions a–e.

1 a flood
2 a hurricane
3 high temperatures
4 droughts
5 rising sea levels

a when it is hotter than normal
b when the level of sea gets higher and covers more land
c long periods when there is little or no rain
d a large amount of water that covers an area which is usually dry
e a violent storm with strong winds

2 Complete the text with the words below.

> hurricanes   sea levels   droughts
> melting   high temperatures ✓
> species   floods

Global Warming

The Earth's climate is changing very quickly because of global warming. These are some of the problems.

Many countries with ¹ _high temperatures_ have no water and are suffering from ² _____.

Other places have too much rain and the water causes ³ _____.

Lots of animals are in danger. Giant pandas, blue whales and tigers are just some of the ⁴ _____ that are in danger.

Every year there are violent storms and ⁵ _____ which destroy towns and villages.

⁶ _____ ice at the North Pole is causing rising ⁷ _____.

The world has to do something soon!

Grammar

Present perfect with *for* and *since*

3 (＊) Complete the expressions with *for* or *since*.

1 _for_ five months
2 _____ three seconds
3 _____ 8.30
4 _____ 2006
5 _____ last summer
6 _____ a week

4 (＊) Underline the correct word to complete the sentences.

1 There have been eight serious hurricanes every year *for/since* almost twenty years.
2 The Earth's temperature has risen by 1°C *for/since* 1900.
3 It hasn't rained in parts of Australia *for/since* the late 1990s.
4 The floods in India have been more serious *for/since* the past few years.
5 It has been impossible to farm in parts of Australia *for/since* several years.
6 There have been fewer polar bears and penguins *for/since* 1987.

5 (＊) Complete the sentences with the present perfect of the verbs in brackets with *for* or *since*.

1 Laura _hasn't visited_ (not/visit) her hometown _since_ Christmas.
2 Jill _____ (live) in Italy _____ ten months.
3 Maria _____ (not/study) English _____ last year.
4 Gary _____ (not/see) his cousin _____ two years.
5 A: How long _____ (you/know) Garry?
   B: _____ 2006.
6 Carrie and Roberto _____ (be) penfriends _____ last summer.

6 (＊＊) Use the prompts to make questions with *How long …?* Then answer the questions using *since* and *for*.

1 know/your best friend?

   How long have you known your best friend?
   I've known him/her since we were at primary school.

2 lived/in the house where you live now?

   _____
   _____

3 be/at your school?

   _____
   _____

4 have/your favourite possession?

   _____
   _____

7 (***) Complete the text with the present perfect or past simple of the verbs in brackets and *for* or *since*.

Fighting hail!

Hail is small balls of ice that falls from the sky. [1]_____ centuries many people [2]_____ (think) that hailstorms happen in winter because the rain turns to ice but that is wrong. Most hailstorms happen in summer when the air near the Earth is warm enough for thunderstorms, but the air higher up is cold enough for ice.

[3]_____ many years hailstorms [4]_____ (destroy) crops and land. [5]_____ 2008 the government of Himachal Pradesh in India [6]_____ (try) to find a solution because they [7]_____ (want) to help the local farmers. Now they are looking at a new technology to help protect farmers from the terrible hailstorms in the area. They want to use special guns to destroy the hail.

The idea of anti-hail guns is not new. Scientists [8]_____(study) the possibilities [9]_____ the 1800s. They [10]___(know) [11]_____ decades that strong waves of air from a gun into the air creates pressure, that can turn the hail into rain. Farmers in parts of France [12]_____ (use) them in the 1970s, but they [13]_____ (not be) very successful. Now, scientist [14]_____ (develop) a better anti-hail gun. Maybe it can help farmers, not only in India but all over the world!

Grammar Plus: Adjectives with *very* and *absolutely*

8 (**) Complete the sentences with *very* or *absolutely*.

There was a [1] *very* bad hurricane last month, the winds were [2]_____ terrible and the waves were [3]_____ enormous all along the coast. After the hurricane there were [4]_____ serious floods in some places. The year before it was [5]_____ hot all summer and the high temperatures were [6]_____ awful. I saw a(n) [7]_____ incredible hailstorm – it was [8]_____ frightening.

Grammar reference

Present perfect with *for* and *since*

We use the present perfect to talk about an action that started in the past and continues into the present.
I've known Milly for ten years.
We've lived in this house since 2005.

> **Notice!**
> If the action is finished, we must use the past simple:
> *Shakespeare **lived** in London most of his life.*
> (= he is dead so the action is finished)
> *I **worked** with Kerry between 2005 and 2007.*
> (= this period is finished)
> Compare this with the present perfect.
> *I've lived in London for five years.* (= I still live in London)
> *I've worked with Kerry for ages.* (= I still work with Kerry)

We often use *for* and *since* with unfinished past actions.

• We use *for* with **periods** of time.
*Dan's **worked** in the company **for seventeen years**.*
*I've **been** ill **for a few days**.*

Other phrases that go with *for*:
for ten minutes, for three months, for hundreds of years, for a long time

• We use *since* with **points** in time.
*I've been in this class **since last September**.*
*We've had this car **since 2006**.*

Other phrases that go with *since*:
since 8.00, since yesterday, since last Friday, since 1998, since I was born

• We can also use phrases like *all day, all week, all my life* with the present perfect to describe unfinished actions:
*I've **lived** in this town **all my life**.*
*My mum's **been** really ill **all week**.*

• We often ask questions with *How long ...?* and the present perfect.
*How long **have** you **known** Tom?*
*How long **has** he **lived** here?*

Vocabulary

The biggest bang in history

1a Write the noun forms of the verbs.

1 explain _explanation_

2 disappear _____

3 destroy _____

4 explode _____

5 crash _____

6 inspire _____

7 smoke _____

8 erupt _____

b Find the nouns from exercise 1a. Look → and ↓ .

d	e	s	t	r	u	c	t	i	o	n
i	x	t	y	j	n	r	m	n	m	v
s	p	g	d	s	a	a	z	s	x	c
a	l	q	w	r	t	s	t	p	h	j
p	o	z	x	c	b	h	n	i	b	n
p	s	m	o	k	e	u	i	r	o	l
e	i	a	p	b	u	g	c	a	n	m
a	o	z	l	j	h	k	o	t	v	p
r	n	i	o	g	q	o	d	i	e	q
a	w	w	m	r	r	m	f	o	a	j
n	e	q	g	e	u	k	r	n	m	k
c	e	r	u	p	t	i	o	n	h	j
e	x	p	l	a	n	a	t	i	o	n

2 Complete the sentences with the words below.

> shake   destroy   explosion
> volcanic eruption ✓   ash   gunfire
> uninhabited island   sailing ship   loud noise

1 Many people died in Pompeii when there was a _volcanic eruption._

2 Natural disasters often _____ everything around them.

3 Columns of _____ and smoke explode into the sky when a volcano erupts.

4 Lots of people dream about living on an _____ but it might be very dangerous.

5 When the volcano exploded, we heard a _____ . It was louder than an _____or _____ . Everyone started to _____ with fear.

6 They crossed the ocean in a _____ .

Reading

3 Look at the photos and read the title of the text and the first paragraph. Choose the best answer.

1 The text is

a a magazine article with interviews.

b two diary extracts by disaster survivors.

DISA

Every year, thousands of people's lives are affected by disasters. This week, in News Magazine two disaster survivors, Jamie King and Fiona Jones, tell us their stories.

Jamie King

NM: Jamie, you were in an air disaster.
1 ___

JK: Two months ago. We were flying home after a holiday on a Greek island and then disaster struck.

NM: 2 ___

JK: We were only in the air for a few minutes, we could still see the coast below. Suddenly there was an explosion and then two seconds later we heard another explosion. I looked out of the window and I could see a lot of smoke. The engine was on fire! Then the plane started to go down.

NM: 3 ___

JK: I was absolutely terrified! Lots of people started screaming and crying. We were very lucky. The man who was flying the plane was an excellent pilot. We crashed into the water, but the plane didn't sink. Everyone was able to get out of the plane.

4 Read the text and match the missing questions to the gaps in the text 1–7. There is one question you do not need.

a Have you flown since then?

b What happened?

c And what happened after the cyclone?

d What did you do when the cyclone arrived?

e When did it happen?

f How did you feel?

g Where did you sleep that night?

h Where was that?

5 Read the text again. Tick (✓) true or cross (✗) false.

1 ☐ The plane disaster happened near the island.

2 ☐ They had to wait a long time for the ships to arrive.

3 ☐ Jamie hates flying now.

4 ☐ Three crocodiles attacked a car.

5 ☐ It will probably cost around $110,000,000 to repair the damage.

6 ☐ Weather experts think the weather will get better.

STER!

NM: Did you have to wait long to be rescued?

JK: No, because we were so close to land, some ships arrived very quickly and rescued us. We went to hospital and then to a hotel.

NM: 4 ___

JK: Yes! We had to get on a plane to go home the next day. I was a bit worried, but it was fine. The funny thing is that I used to hate flying. Now I don't mind it, I think: 'The worst has happened. I was in a crash and I survived.'

Fiona Jones

NM: Fiona, you were in a cyclone. **5** ___

FJ: In north Australia, in Normanton. That's where I live.

NM: 6 ___

FJ: We all stayed inside, in the basement, because that's the safest place. We could hear the storm coming closer and closer. The noise was awful. At one point there was a really loud noise. I thought: 'That's it! It's going to destroy the house!' I was shaking.

NM: 7 ___

FJ: There were terrible floods. More than 360 millimetres of rain fell in just twenty-four hours. The army had to bring food and water to the whole area by plane and helicopter. The strangest thing was that waves from the coast and rivers flooded the land and carried three crocodiles to near my house! One of my neighbours hit a crocodile with his car – it was 1.6 metres long.

NM: Really? That's incredible! So is everything back to normal again now?

FJ: Not really. The floods have gone, but they destroyed a lot of homes and farms. It's going to cost at least 110 million dollars to repair the damage.

NM: So is the weather usually this bad?

FJ: No, but this summer was very hot. If it stays hot, there will probably be another cyclone. All the experts say that the extreme temperatures and heavy rain will only increase because of climate change.

Reading

Gapped text

1 Read the first paragraph of a brochure about Arizona. What do you think the whole text will be about?

a the desert scenery   **b** cowboys
c different places in Arizona

When we think about Arizona, we first think about cowboys riding on horseback across the desert among cactus plants the size of trees. But Arizona has a great variety of scenery, climate, plant life and wildlife.

2 Match 1–4 with a–d to make sentences. <u>Underline</u> the words that connect the beginning and ending of each sentence grammatically.

1 The Four Corners is the place
2 Navajo and Anasazi Indians used
3 In Arizona you can see 60 percent of all the animal species
4 The Colorado river is shorter

a than the Mississippi.
b that live in the United States.
c to build houses inside caves.
d <u>where</u> four states meet at one point; these are Colorado, New Mexico, Arizona and Utah.

3 Read the second paragraph of the text. Complete the gaps with a phrase from a–c below. There is one extra phrase.

The Mountain Region is the name of several mountain ranges ¹ _____ . The highest peak, Mount Humphreys, is 3,852 metres high ² _____ .

a that cross the state from the northwest to the southeast.
b and there is snow at the top even in the summer.
c and it is very popular with swimmers.

4 Read the rest of the brochure. Complete each gap with a phrase from a–f below. There is one extra phrase.

The desert region in the south-west is not an empty, dry area of sand ¹ _____ . Many species of plants and animals live there. It is also the part of Arizona ² _____ .

The north-eastern plains contain some of Arizona's most spectacular sights, among them the incredible ruins of Navajo Indian houses, the Painted Desert and the Petrified Forest with trees ³ _____ . The most famous sight of all is the Grand Canyon, created by the Colorado river. The Canyon is more ⁴ _____ . When you look down its 1,000 metre walls, you can see two billion years of the Earth's history in the rocks.

Another unusual place in Arizona is the Meteor Crater, where a nickel-iron meteorite weighing about 300,000 tons hit the Earth about 50,000 years ago. It caused an explosion ⁵ _____ . The crater is more than a kilometre wide and 170 metres deep.

a than 400 kilometres long and from six to twenty-nine kilometres wide.
b like many other deserts.
c which melted rocks and destroyed all life within about three to four kilometres.
d and it became a national park in 1919.
e where most of the state's cities are located.
f that turned to stone about 200 million years ago.

Listening

True/False

5 Read the pairs of sentences. Tick (✓) if they mean the same and cross (✗) if they don't.

1 ☐ I bought it on Saturday./I've had it since Saturday.
2 ☐ It's longer than I thought./It's not as long as I thought.
3 ☐ I don't know./I'm not sure.

6 (12) **Listen to the conversation. Tick (✓) true or cross (✗) false.**

1 ☐ The customer has had the phone since last Thursday.

2 ☐ The customer is sure which part of the phone is causing the problem.

3 ☐ The battery does not work as long as the booklet says.

4 ☐ The customer didn't plug the phone in correctly.

5 ☐ The shop assistant offers to exchange the phone.

Use of English

Gap fill

7 **Complete the exam tip with the words below.**

[who a ✓ be but for her in to]

Exam TIP

The missing words in an exercise with gaps can include:
Articles ¹ __a__ , (*an* or *the*) before nouns, ² ____ before an infinitive (for example in *learn to use, hope to go*)
Prepositions, for example *on, since*, ³ ____ , ⁴ ____
Linking words, for example *and, when*, ⁵ ____ .
Pronouns such as *he, she, him*, ⁶ ____
Relative pronouns such as *which*, ⁷ ____ or *where*
Auxiliary verbs: *do, have*, ⁸ ____ in various forms.

8 **Complete the text with words from exercise 7. You may need to change the form of some of the verbs. You do not need all the words.**

Long time no see

Last week I decided to visit a place on the coast where I used ¹ ____ go on holiday when I was a child. It hasn't changed much ² ____ then. I ³ ____ walking along the sea, looking at the waves, when ⁴ ____ young woman came up to me. 'Excuse me,' she asked. '⁵ ____ you Ginny Crawford?' 'Yes, I am,' I answered and then I remembered. She was the little girl ⁶ ____ lived in the house by the beach, the girl I used to play with when we were both five years old. I remembered her name: Lily. I was very happy to see ⁷ ____ again. We went to a small café ⁸ ____ we used to have ice-cream as children, ⁹ ____ this time we had coffee. We talked ¹⁰ ____ three hours and Lily promised to visit me in London ¹¹ ____ September. ¹² ____ she comes, I'll invite her to my favourite restaurant.

Speaking

Discussing a topic using photos

Exam TIP

When you have to discuss a topic presented in two photos, talk about *both* photos and include *all* the points in the task.

9 **Read the exam task and match sentences 1–9 to the bullet points.**

Look at these photos of people using technology in different ways. Compare and contrast the photos and give your ideas. Include the following points:
- technology used for work and for fun
- good and bad aspects for young people
- the role of technology in your life

1 Both photos show people using technology, but they are using it in different ways.

2 I also use technology for both work and play.

3 Technology can be very good for young people.

4 In the photo on the right, the man is probably working.

5 The people in the first photo are using technology for fun.

6 But it can also be bad.

7 But the most important thing for me is keeping in touch with friends.

8 For example, some people waste a lot of time playing games, chatting on the Internet or sending silly messages.

9 I can't imagine my life without technology.

Vocabulary & Grammar

1 <u>Underline</u> the correct words.

1 Can I borrow your <u>*digital camera*</u>/*hairdryer*? I'd like to take a picture here.
2 Switch the radio *off*/*up*, please. I'm studying.
3 It rains a lot here – we often have *droughts*/*floods*.
4 Your radio isn't broken. First, you need to *plug*/*switch* it in, and then turn it on.
5 The waves in the *sea*/*river* are very big.
6 To start the machine, just *charge*/*press* this button.

/5

2 Complete the sentences with one word in each gap. You can see the first letter of each word.

1 The largest active volcano on the E<u>*arth*</u> today is the Mauna Lau in the Hawaiian islands.
2 Can you s_____ the time on my new watch, please.
3 Dinosaurs became e_____ millions of years ago.
4 My favourite g_____ is my mobile phone.
5 I want to spend a week on an u_____ island. Just me and nature!
6 Scientists are studying the effects of a volcanic e_____ .

/5

3 Complete the definitions with a noun from below and *that, which, who* or *where*. There are three extra nouns.

> remote control   accountant   jungle   field
> games console   shop assistant✓   customer
> answering machine   desert

1 A/An <u>*shop assistant*</u> is a person <u>*who*</u> sells things in a shop.
2 A/An _____ is a place _____ it is always very hot and dry.
3 A/An _____ is a gadget _____ is used to control a machine from a distance.
4 A/An _____ is a place _____ you can find tropical trees and wild animals.
5 A/An _____ is someone _____ buys things.
6 A/An _____ is a gadget _____ records messages left by callers.

/5

4 Write sentences in the present perfect tense using the prompts in brackets. Add *for* or *since* where necessary.

1 (It/ not rain/here/2006)
   <u>*It hasn't rained here since 2006.*</u>
2 (They/be/at school/8 o'clock)
   _____
3 (I/not talk/to Martha/a long time)
   _____
4 (How long/you/know/him/?)
   _____
5 (We/not see/our teacher/Christmas)
   _____
6 (Lee/live/in France/five years)
   _____

/5

5 <u>Underline</u> the correct forms.

1 *I don't lend/<u>won't lend</u>* you my dress if you don't ask me politely.
2 She'll text me when her bus *arrives/will arrive*.
3 If you don't give me her telephone number, I *won't be able to/am not able to* contact her.
4 If the weather *is/will be* fine, we'll go out.
5 I'll cook dinner before they *come/will come*.
6 If Paul *doesn't come/won't come* back before 11 p.m., his parents will be very worried.

/5

6 Correct the mistakes in the sentences.

1 One day Nick used to bring his dog to school.
   <u>*One day Nick brought his dog to school.*</u>
2 It use to snow a lot in this part of the country.
   _____
3 The temperature here yesterday used to be very high.
   _____
4 When the children heard an explosion, they used to scream with fear.
   _____
5 Did your father used to play football when he was a teenager?
   _____
6 We didn't used to fly but now we go by plane everywhere.
   _____

/5

Reading

7 Read the text about Hurricane Ike and Gustav. Choose the correct answer.

Hurricane Ike and Gustav: the damage to Cuba

Hurricane Ike hit eastern Cuba with enormous waves and very heavy rain last night. Ike hit Cuba only a week after Hurricane Gustav caused bad floods and destruction in many areas. Experts say that £2.8 billion is needed to build new houses and help the people. Four hundred and fifty thousand homes were affected. At least two hundred thousand Cubans have lost their homes and a huge amount of farming land has been destroyed.

There are also hundreds of people who desperately need somewhere to stay for a few weeks. These people have no electricity or water in their homes, so they cannot live in them at the moment. Los Palacios in the western area of Pinar del Rio experienced some of the strongest winds of the hurricane: winds of 150 miles per hour hit the seashore, and huge waves crashed onto the shore. The strength of the winds blew lots of houses and shops away into the sea – total destruction in many areas. One local shop owner from Los Palacios, Rosa, told us about the storm: 'My family went to our local church to be safe from the hurricanes. It was terrifying …, we heard loud crashes and noises as the winds destroyed buildings. Some of my friends went to special shelters to stay warm and safe – we have these shelters for bad weather conditions. I can't believe the terrible destruction … . Miraculously, all the people of Los Palacios are okay, with only some injuries. It was good to see people helping other people: young people got food, water and warm blankets for us. I was thankful. I believe that our people's strength will help Cuba in the next few weeks and months.

1 Hurricane Gustav hit Cuba _____ Hurricane Ike.

   a before   **b** after   **c** at the same time as

2 The cost of the storms for the island is

   a £450,000.   **b** £200,000.   **c** £2,800,000,000.

3 Many people are without _____ in their homes.

   a water   **b** electricity   **c** water and electricity

4 In Los Palacios

   a many buildings disappeared into the sea.

   b the winds were weaker than in other areas.

   c the waves were not strong.

5 Rosa's family stayed in a nearby _____ during the hurricanes.

   a special shelter   **b** shop   **c** church

6 In Rosa's opinion, people in Los Palacios

   a gave each other a lot of support during the hurricanes.

   b are not strong enough to recover from the hurricanes.

   c will need more food, water and blankets after the hurricanes.

/6

Communication

8 Complete the dialogues with the words and phrases below.

> I'd like   exchange it   refund   work properly
> problem   receipt   there's nothing
> keep it   speak to   help you ✓

1 A: Hello, can I ¹ _help you_?
   B: Yes, I bought this CD player here two days ago and it doesn't ² _____ .
      I'd like a ³ _____ , please.
   A: Have you got the ⁴ _____ ?
   B: No, I didn't ⁵ _____ .
   A: I'm afraid we can't give refunds if you don't have the receipt. But we can ⁶ _____ if you like.
   B: I'm really not happy about this. Could I ⁷ _____ the manager, please?

2 A: What exactly is the ⁸ _____ ?
   B: I bought this dress here in a sale and it has a big stain on it. ⁹ _____ my money back.
   A: I'm afraid ¹⁰ _____ I can do. We never give refunds for clothes bought in a sale.

/9

9 Complete the instructions with one word in each gap. You can see the first letter of each word.

How to ¹u_se_ a games console for the first time

² F_____ of all, you switch on the system.
³ T_____ you wait for the language selection screen to appear. You ⁴ h_____ to use the control pad to select a language. ⁵ J_____ follow the instructions on the screen. When you finish setting up your games console for the first time, it will shut down automatically to save your settings. Enjoy playing games but ⁶ d_____ forget to take a break from time to time!

/5

Marks

Vocabulary & Grammar	/30 marks
Reading	/6 marks
Communication	/14 marks
Total:	/50 marks

must see

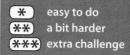

* easy to do
** a bit harder
*** extra challenge

Vocabulary

Making a film

1 Match the films A–E with the descriptions 1–5.

A *Elizabeth The Golden Age*
a film about Elizabeth I of England

B **Notting Hill**
a film about an ordinary boy who falls in love with a famous film star

C **Friday 13th**
a series of films where groups of people die in frightening circumstances

D **STAR WARS**
a series of films set in space

E **The Bourne Trilogy**
a series of films with lots of action and suspense

1 [b] romantic comedy
2 [ ] thriller
3 [ ] horror
4 [ ] historical drama
5 [ ] fantasy/science fiction

2 Complete the sentences with the words below.

publicity   script   special effects   scenes
actors   budget   director   stars ✓

1 Top *stars* earn enormous amounts of money for a film.

2 _____ are used a lot in science fiction films.

3 A _____ is the person who tells the actors what to do.

4 Film companies spend money on _____ . They make posters and adverts for the films called 'trailers'.

5 The _____ in a film are filmed in any order because they are edited afterwards.

6 The story and the lines that the actors have to learn is called the _____ .

7 The _____ is the amount of money that is available to make a film.

8 _____ are the people who play different parts in the film.

Grammar

Present simple passive

3 (*) Put the words in the correct order to make sentences using the present simple passive.

1 grown/in Colombia/is/a lot of coffee
   A lot of coffee is grown is Colombia.

2 manufactured/Ferrari cars/aren't/in Australia
   _____

3 bicycles/are/how many/every year/stolen/in Amsterdam?
   _____

4 the best watches/made/in Switzerland?/watches/are
   _____

5 the story/the director/by/is/written/?
   _____

6 spoken/English/all over the world/ is
   _____

7 by/chosen/isn't/the actors/the music for the film
   _____

4 (**) Underline the correct forms to complete the text.

Making a film

The script [1] *writes/is written* by film writers and the producer [2] *chooses/is chosen* the director. Then, the actors [3] *choose/are chosen*. After that, the film company [4] *looks/is looked* for the right locations. The actors [5] *do/are done* some scenes on location, but it's very expensive so many scenes [6] *film/are filmed* in the film studios. Special effects [7] *don't add /aren't added* until later. When the film is ready, it [8] *doesn't release/isn't released* to the public immediately. Usually a small group of people [9] *watch/is watched* the film and then the editor and director [10] *make/are made* any final changes.

5 (**✱✱**) Write the quiz questions and then answer the questions. Use the present simple passive.

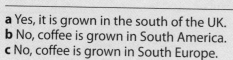

General knowledge quiz

1 where/Harley-Davidson motorcycles/build?

   Where are Harley Davidson motorcycles built?

   a In the UK. **b** In the USA.
   c In Australia.

2 coffee/grow/Britain?

   _____

   a Yes, it is grown in the south of the UK.
   b No, coffee is grown in South America.
   c No, coffee is grown in South Europe.

3 where/the biggest diamond mine/
   in the world/situate?

   _____

   a In Africa. **b** In Australia.
   c In Siberia in Russia.

4 the crown jewels of Britain/keep/Buckingham Palace?

   _____

   a No, they are kept in the Tower of London.
   b Yes, the Queen keeps them under her bed.
   c Yes, they are kept in the palace.

5 where/Volkswagen cars/produce?

   _____

   a In Germany. **b** In Italy. **c** In Switzerland.

   Answers on page 92

6 (**✱✱✱**) Complete the sentences so the meaning is the same. Use the correct form of the present simple passive.

1 Cinemas often show foreign films with subtitles.

   Foreign films with subtitles are often shown in cinemas.

2 People watch foreign language films all over the world.

   Foreign language films _____
   _____ .

3 People don't translate every word from the original script.

   Every word from the original script _____
   _____ .

4 Many countries use the same people to dub the voices of lots of different actors.

   The same people _____
   _____ .

5 Producers shorten the subtitles to make them easier to read.

   Subtitles _____
   _____ .

Grammar reference

Present simple passive

Form

+	I	am ('m) invited.
	We/You/They	are ('re) invited.
	He/She/It	is ('s) invited.
–	I	am not ('m not) invited.
	We/You/They	are not ('re not) invited.
	He/She/It	is not ('s not) invited.
?	Am I	
	Is he/she/it	invited?
	Are we/you/they	

Short answers

Yes, I **am**. / No, I'm **not**.
Yes, he/she/it **is**. / No, he/she/it **isn't**.
Yes, we/you/they **are**. / No, we/you/they **aren't**.

Wh- questions

Where are these cars produced?
How often are newspapers delivered to your house?

Use

• We use the passive when it is not important who does the action, or we are not interested in who does it.

Thousands of people **are expected** to attend the concert. (= it doesn't matter who expects them)
These bags **are made** in Italy. (= it doesn't matter who makes them)

• We also often use the passive when it is obvious who does the action.

Lots of people **are arrested** at football matches. (= obviously the police arrest them)
I'm **not invited** to Joe's party. (= obviously Joe hasn't invited me)

• We can still say who does the action in passive sentences, using by

This car **is made by Renault**.
Thousands of people **are killed by drunk drivers** every year.

Vocabulary

TV programmes

1 What kind of TV programmes do the pictures show? Label the pictures with the words below.

> sports programme ✓ cartoon quiz show
> cookery programme weather forecast
> news

1 <u>sports programme</u> 4 _____

2 _____ 5 _____

3 _____ 6 _____

2 Match the words 1–6 with the definitions a–f.

1 A soap opera
2 An advert
3 The news
4 A documentary
5 A comedy series
6 A reality show

a tries to make us buy a product.

b gives us factual information on different topics.

c is a fictional series about everyday life.

d is a programme where the people aren't actors and they are filmed doing things.

e are programmes about funny situations that try to make us laugh.

f is a programme that tells us what is happening in our country and the rest of the world.

3 Can you think of a programme in your country for each type of programme in exercises 1 and 2?

Grammar

Past simple and present perfect passive

4 (✱) <u>Underline</u> the passive verbs. Are they past simple (PS) or present perfect (PP)?

1 Harry Potter <u>was written</u> by JK Rowling. The first book came out in 1997. _PS_

2 Paul McCartney wrote *Yesterday* when he was only nineteen years old. _____

3 *Big Brother* has been filmed in almost seventy countries so far. _____

4 Bruce Lee was filmed in slow motion because he moved too fast for the camera. _____

5 The Dolby surround stereo system was first used in the movie *Star Wars*. _____

5 (✱) Complete the sentences with the correct form of the past simple passive.

Amazing early film facts!

★ Early films ¹ _were made_ (make) in black and white and they didn't have sound.

★ In the cinema, music ² _____ (play) to accompany the film.

★ In the beginning, films ³ _____ (not shown) in cinemas. They were shown in theatres.

★ The first cinema, called the Nickleodeon, ⁴ _____ (open) in Pittsburgh in 1905.

★ How ⁵ _____ (films/sell)? They ⁶ _____ (sell) by the metre! In the USA they cost around forty-five cents per metre.

★ Some of the first special effects ⁷ _____ (create) by the Edison company.

★ The first animated cartoon ⁸ _____ (not made) until 1908. It was called Fantasmagorie.

6 (✱) Complete the sentences with the correct form of the present perfect passive.

1 Millions of films _have been made_ (make) since the start of cinema.

2 _____ (that film release) on DVD yet?

3 The Oscar winners _____ (not decide) yet, but I think the actors _____ (nominate).

4 How many _____ (films direct) by Steven Spielberg?

5 A: _____ (the actors choose) yet? B: No, but the script _____ (write).

6 The film _____ (translate) into three different languages, but the dubbing _____ (not finish) yet.

7 (✱✱) Complete the sentences about the *Pirates of the Caribbean* films using the correct form of the past simple or present perfect passive.

1 Walt Disney Pictures released *The Curse of the Black Pearl* in 2003.

   The Curse of the Black Pearl <u>was released in 2003 by Walt Disney Pictures</u>.

2 The makers based the film on a theme park ride at Disney theme parks.

   The film _____.

3 The producer rejected the original script.

   The original script _____.

4 The second and third films have broken box office records.

   Box office records _____.

5 The popularity of the films has surprised all the main actors.

   All the main actors _____.

8 (✱✱✱) Read the leaflet about Disney World. Complete the text using the correct form of the verbs in brackets. Use the past simple or the present perfect.

> ### Disney World in Florida
>
> ☆ It's the only theme park which ¹ _____ (design) by Walt Disney.
>
> ☆ It ² _____ (visit) by more than 515 million people since it ³ _____ (open) in 1955.
>
> ☆ Two children ⁴ _____(photograph) with Walt Disney as the first visitors to DisneyWorld and they ⁵_____ (give) special tickets to allow them to go to DisneyWorld whenever they wanted ... forever!!
>
> ☆ The park celebrated its 50th birthday in 2005 and lots of the old funfair rides ⁶ _____ (restore) for this.

Grammar Plus: Time expressions in passive sentences

9 (✱✱✱) Rewrite the sentences with the words in brackets in the correct place.

1 Their last film was finished. (never)

   <u>Their last film was never finished.</u>

2 Music is chosen by specialists. (sometimes)

   _____

3 Reality shows are shown in the evening. (usually)

   _____

4 Special effects are created by computers. (often)

   _____

5 Part three of the film was finished. (never)

   _____

Grammar reference

Past simple and present perfect passive

Past simple passive

To form the past simple passive we use the verb *to be* in the past simple (*was/were*) + the past participle.

Form

+	I/He/She/It	*was arrested.*
	We/You/They	*were arrested.*
−	I/He/She/It	*was not (wasn't) arrested.*
	We/You/They	*were not (weren't) arrested.*
?	*Was* I/he/she/it *Were* we/you/they	*invited?*

Short answers

Yes, I/he/she/it **was**. */ No, I/he/she/it* **wasn't**.
Yes, we/you/they **were**. */ No, we/you/they* **weren't**.

Wh- questions

When was the Internet invented?
Where was this programme recorded?

Present perfect passive

To form the present perfect passive we use the verb *to be* in the present perfect (*have/has been*) + the past participle.

Form

+	I/We/You/They	*have been arrested.*
	He/She/It	*has been arrested.*
−	I/We/You/They	*have not (haven't) been arrested.*
	He/She/It	*has not (hasn't) been arrested.*
?	*Have* I/we/you/they *Has* he/she/it	*been invited?*

Short answers

Yes, I/we/you/they **have**. */ No, I/we/you/they* **haven't**.
Yes, he/she/it **has**. */ No, he/she/it* **hasn't**.

Wh- questions

Why haven't I been invited to Sara's party?
Where have the criminals been taken?

Vocabulary

Describing books and films

1 Complete the sentences with the words below.

> novel   magazines ✓   poetry   comics
> newspaper   short stories   blog

1 I like reading geographic _magazines_ because they have interesting articles about various places in the world and great photographs.

2 A lot of children like _____ because they enjoy the stories and pictures.

3 I have started writing a _____ on the Internet about my life.

4 I think it must be difficult to write _____ because you have to really think about the meaning of the words.

5 I'm reading a great _____ . The characters and events are not real, but it's very good.

6 Most people read the _____ in the morning to find out what has happened in the world.

7 I prefer reading _____ to long books because you can read them quite quickly.

2 Complete the description of Ellie's favourite book with the words and phrases below.

> was written by   was released   is called ✓
> stars   It's set   favourite part   characters
> it's about   I like it because

My favourite book [1] _is called_ Eragon. [2] _____ in an imaginary country and [3] _____ a boy called Eragon who finds an egg in the forest. He takes it home and a dragon comes out of it. In the story, the [4] _____ are trying to save their country. [5] _____ the story is full of adventure and magic. It [6] _____ a writer called Christopher Paolini.

The book has also been made into a film. The film [7] _____ in 2006 and it [8] _____ Edward Speleers, Jeremy Irons and Robert Carlyle. They are great actors! My [9] _____ is when Eragon flies on his dragon, Saphira, for the first time.

Listening

3 ⟨13⟩ You are going to listen to five short interviews. Listen to the introduction and choose the best answer.

1 The interviewer is doing the survey
  a in the street.   b in a TV studio.   c in a school.

4 ⟨13⟩ Read the opinions a–g. Then listen to the street survey again and match the speakers 1–5 with their opinions a–g. There are two extra opinions.

1 Jamie   4 Mr Brown
2 Lisa   5 Chris
3 Valerie

a Adverts try to make people buy things that they don't need.

b Most adverts aren't very interesting, particularly adverts for things like shampoo.

c They shouldn't have adverts during films on television. It's annoying.

d You can learn a lot from adverts about different products.

e Children shouldn't watch TV adverts, it just makes them want more toys.

f It's a good thing to have the same adverts on many times, it helps you remember them.

g Adverts are okay, but they last too long and they shouldn't be on so often.

5 ⟨13⟩ Listen to the interviews again. Tick (✓) true or cross (✗) false.

1 ☐ The interviewer is doing the survey in London.

2 ☐ Jamie likes adverts for cars.

3 ☐ Lisa likes adverts in the cinema.

4 ☐ Valerie always listens carefully to all the adverts.

5 ☐ Mr Brown watches TV channels that don't have adverts.

6 ☐ Chris enjoys watching film trailers on TV.

Reading

6 Look at the texts A–E and match them to the correct description 1–5.

1 ☐ Information about what's on at a cinema

2 ☐ Advert for a film

3 ☐ Film blog

4 ☐ Extract from a TV guide

5 ☐ Description of a film from a book about films

7 Read the texts and answer the questions.

1 Who is the writer of *Rachel Getting Married*?

_____

2 How much does a student ticket cost at the Odeon Cinema?

_____

3 How many performances of *Bride Wars* are there each day?

_____

4 What kind of programme is *Rosa*?

_____

5 Who was *Slumdog Millionaire* directed by?

_____

6 In the book *Slam*, what is the main character's favourite sport?

_____

8 Read the texts. Tick (✓) true, cross (✗) false or write (?) if the text doesn't say.

1 ☐ Kim hasn't met Rachel's future husband before.

2 ☐ A cinema ticket for a ten-year old costs four pounds.

3 ☐ If you want to book a cinema ticket, you must do it on the Internet.

4 ☐ There are no programmes for sports fans on Thursday.

5 ☐ The film poster says that *Slumdog Millionaire* has won ten Oscars.

6 ☐ *Slam* has already been translated into Japanese.

A

Rachel Getting Married
(USA, 2008. 1 hour 54 min.) Drama.
Directed by Jonathan Demme.

Stars Anne Hathaway, Rosemarie DeWitt, Debra Winger

Kim has some big problems. She returns home for her sister Rachel's wedding. Soon, we discover a lot of old family secrets.

Rachel Getting Married presents a funny picture of family life. The characters are very well done and first-time writer Jenny Lumet's dialogues are very realistic. The actors are excellent.

B

ODEON CINEMA

This week's performances are listed below. For further information, ring 01207 543 776.

Tickets: £5.50 (adults), £4 (children under 12 and over 65s), £4.50 (students).

Book tickets online (www.odeoncinema23.com) or by phone (902 226134).

Revolutionary Road *Screen 1:* 16.10, 18.10, 20.20, 22.30

Bride Wars *Screen 2:* 17.45, 19.40, 21.45

High School Musical 3 *Screen 3:* 16.05, 18.10, 20.20

Madagascar 2 *Screen 4:* 14.30, 16.30, 18.15, 20.10

Late night performances Friday and Saturday:
Vicky Christina Barcelona *Screen 4:* 22.30, 0.30

C

Thursday's programmes

14.30 **World of Nature.** Documentary about African Wildlife.
15.50 **Rosa.** Soap Opera with Natalie Young and Rob Martin.
17.30 **The Simpsons.** Bart and Lisa fight over the TV remote control … and suddenly they become part of a TV programme!
18.00 **News and Weather.**
19.30 **Numbers and Letters.** Quiz programme with Matthew Taylor.
20.20 **Football.** Live England v Brazil game.

D

"THE **FEEL-GOOD** FILM OF THE **DECADE**"
★★★★★

SLUMDOG MILLIONAIRE A FILM BY DANNY BOYLE

E

Good news! DNA films are going to do a film version of Nick Hornby's book *Slam*. *Slam* is about a sixteen-year-old boy called Sam who loves skateboarding. Sam's hero is professional skateboarder Tony Hawk. Sam talks to Tony (well, the poster of Tony on his bedroom wall) about his problems. Life has got better for Sam recently – his mum has stopped seeing her awful boyfriend (Sam's parents are divorced), he's getting on well with his dad and he's learned some great new skating tricks. Then he meets Alicia and they start going out … and then the problems start. I won't tell you any more or it'll spoil the story!

The book's already been translated into twenty-six languages, including Croatian, Finnish and Korean, but not Japanese yet, and it's popular with young people.

Julia

Writing

Adverts and notices

1 Read the adverts and notices and answer the questions.

1 What has Mike lost? What does it look like?

_____

2 What is Ruth offering?

_____

3 How much is the room in Marek's apartment?

_____

4 How is Clara planning to travel to Stratford?

_____

5 What kind of animal has Jan found? What does it look like?

_____

2 Read the adverts and notices again and write the abbreviations for the words below.

1 tickets _____ _tckts_
2 weekends _____
3 non-smoker _____
4 mobile _____
5 minutes _____
6 as soon as possible _____
7 year-old _____
8 per hour _____

1 Give your advert or notice a title.

2 Give details such as the date or description. You can write the day in full or give the short form (*Mon, Tues, Weds, Thurs, Fri, Sat, Sun*). If you are selling something, give the price.

LOST!!
MP3 player with silver and black case
Lost in sports centre on Tues 12 June
£10 reward!
If you've found it, please contact Mike
on 01024 653378

3 Say who to contact and give the number. Use *Call/ Phone/Contact* + name. For a mobile number use *mob* (= mobile).

4 For classes give the cost per hour: *£20 p.h.*

SNOWBOARDING LESSONS AVAILABLE
Individual or small groups – wknds only
£20–£30 p.h.
Experienced teacher – classes for all ages
Phone Ruth on 548 44 23 09
(mob 653762991)

5 If you are offering something, for example you are looking for a roommate or selling something, you can begin with a question to get people's interest: *Looking for a new guitar? Need a room to rent?*

ROOM FOR RENT
Looking for accommodation near Styles College?
Nice, big room available in apartment 10 mins
walk from the college and near shops and public
transport (underground 15 mins and buses 35, 76).
I'm a 23 yr old Polish student, who likes music,
photography and walking. N/S pls.
£85 p.w.
Call Marek on 01207 3547988

6 You can use abbreviations in your adverts/notices: *N/S* = non-smoker (someone who doesn't smoke), *mins* = minutes, *pls* = please.

7 Give prices for rooms per week: *(p.w.)*

8 You can miss out the verb *be*, pronouns and articles: write *Cost around £30* instead of *The cost is around £30.*

TRIP TO STRATFORD
I'm organising trip to visit Shakespeare's
birthplace and see Romeo and Juliet wknd
26–27 March.
Cost around £30 for transport (train) plus £25
for night in youth hostel. Tckts for play £30.
Interested?
Call Clara on 0141 798532 a.s.a.p.
(mob 07189 55341)

FOUND
Small black and white
cat with red collar
found in area near
Brown's Internet café
Please contact Jan on
0788 124357

3 Write full sentences from the advert and notice phrases below.

1 Want to go on trip to Stratford?

   Do you want to go on a trip to Stratford?

2 Need classes in Maths or Physics?

   _____

3 Can give classes evs or at wknd.

   _____

4 Lost blue mobile phone.

   _____

5 Looking for a room to rent?

   _____

6 Organising trip to London next Sat.

   _____

4 Read the task and then read Marek's advert on page 98 again. What information does he *not* include?

You are doing a language course in the UK and you are looking for a roommate. Write an advert. In the advert:

• explain why you are writing,

• describe your apartment and its location,

• write information about yourself (nationality, interests, character qualities),

• explain what kind of person you would like to share the apartment with.

5 Complete the strategies box with the words below.

[unnecessary ✓   pronouns   title
  contact details]

Adverts and notices

• Decide what information you need to include.
• Make notes for your advert or notice. Choose the things you need to say. Don't include ¹ *unnecessary* information.
• Write the advert/notice. You can miss out the verb *to be*, ² _____ and articles.
• Remember to include some ³ _____ .
• Give your advert/notice a ⁴ _____ .

6 Read the task and write your advert. Use the strategies in exercise 5 to help you.

You are on a language course in London. You are looking for people who would like to go on a trip to Oxford at the weekend with you. Write a short advert to put on the school notice board. In the advert:

• say that you are looking for students who want to go on a trip,

• include details about the trip (when it is, where it is to, how long it is, how much it costs, how you will travel),

• write how to get in touch with you.

Speaking

Making phone calls

7 Put the telephone conversation in the correct order.

B: ☐ Typical Josh! I'll tell him to call you as soon as he can.

B: ☐ I'm sorry but he isn't here at the moment. Why don't you try his mobile?

A: ☐1 Hi. Could I speak to Josh, please?

A: ☐ Thanks. Bye for now.

A: ☐5 Well, I've already tried but there's no answer. Can you take a message for him?

B: ☐ Yes, just a minute, I'll get him.

A: ☐ Thank you …

B: ☐ Of course. Who's calling?

A: ☐ It's David. Could you tell him that he left his iPod at my flat last night?

8 Complete the dialogue with the phrases below.

[Speak to you soon   Natalie speaking ✓
  Is Fiona there?   why don't you try her mobile?
  she isn't here at the moment.]

Natalie: Hi, ¹ *Natalie speaking*

Eddie: Hi, Natalie, it's Eddie. ² _____

Natalie: Hi, Eddie. I'm sorry, ³ _____.
         Can I take a message?

Eddie: Yes, please. Can you tell her that I got the tickets for the cinema tonight and that I'll meet her there at 7.30?

Natalie: Sure, Eddie. I'll tell her. Listen,
         ⁴ _____ . She's got it with her.

Eddie: Great idea, Natalie, I'll do that now. Thanks. ⁵ _____.

Natalie: Bye for now, Eddie.

12 stay safe

✱	easy to do
✱✱	a bit harder
✱✱✱	extra challenge

Vocabulary

Serious crimes?

1 Read the newspaper extracts and complete the gaps with the words below.

> vandalism   fake ID   speeding   burglary ✓
> dropping litter   playing truant   attacking
> robbery   downloading music illegally
> shoplifting

Police arrest three men

Police arrested three men last night for ¹ _burglary._ The men have stolen money, TVs and computers from over eighty houses in the last month.

Bank drama!

There was a ² _____ in a bank in town yesterday. A man stole $100,000 but his car broke down and he was caught by police.

School ³ _____

Two teenagers are in trouble after they broke windows at a local school and wrote on the walls with paint.

Are our roads safe?

The number of people who drive too fast is increasing. ⁴ _____ is becoming a serious problem.

'⁵ _____ is a big problem,' say shop managers

The Amdale centre loses thousands of pounds every year because people take things without paying. Police were called after two teens tried to steal DVDs yesterday. The teens were ⁶ _____ . They didn't go to class in the afternoon and went to the shopping centre instead.

New under 18s disco

A club plans to have a special early evening disco for young people every Saturday from 7–10.30 p.m. to try to stop young people using ⁹ _____ to get into the over 18s club nights.

Grammar

Second conditional

2 ✱ Match 1–6 with a–f to make sentences in the second conditional.

1 Brian and Craig wouldn't
2 If Jo wanted to go out on a school night,
3 Wendy would use her father's car
4 If Harry tried shoplifting,
5 What would you do
6 If I found ten euros in the street,

a if he gave her permission.
b his parents would be furious.
c I would keep it.
d she would have to ask her parents.
e play truant. They love school.
f if you saw a crime?

3 ✱✱ Underline the correct forms to complete the sentences.

1 Tom *tried/would try* to get into an '18' film if he *looked/would look* older.

2 If there *was/would be* a disco for sixteen to eighteen-year-olds, young people *didn't use/ wouldn't try to use* fake IDs.

3 What *did you do/would you do* if someone *offered/would offer* you a stolen computer?

4 Naomi *didn't feel/wouldn't feel* comfortable if her boyfriend *drove/would drive* over the speed limit.

5 If Tim *didn't listen/wouldn't listen* to free music on the Internet, he *was/would be* unhappy.

City centre cameras see everything

Cameras in the city centre have helped police catch criminals. A man was arrested for ⁷ _____ an old lady. The lady was taken to hospital. Officials also say that the cameras can see people who drop papers and other things on the ground. These people could have to pay a fine for ⁸ _____ .

Make music cheaper!

A survey has shown that people would stop ¹⁰ _____ on their computers if websites reduced the cost of buying music online.

4 (**) Read Kevin's blog and complete the text using the correct form of the second conditional.

Hi there everyone,

I'm in a very bad mood today. I watched a documentary on TV last night about teenage crime. I was really angry about it! They said teenagers do a lot of bad things, but I ¹ _wouldn't do_ (not do) those things, even if someone ² _____ (pay) me! I mean, ³ _____ (you/attack) someone in the street if you ⁴ _____ (know) they had a lot of money? If you ⁵ ____ (drive) your parents' car ⁶ _____ (you/speed) around town? Of course not! Oh, and I ⁷ _____ (not steal) a new laptop or iPod if my old one ⁸ _____ (break down)!!

Most teenagers are good people!

Kevin

5 (***) Write what you would and wouldn't do if these situations happened to you.

What would you do if …

1 you saw a group of young people writing graffiti on a new building?

I wouldn't say anything.
I would tell the owner of the building.

2 your best friend copied from you in an exam?

_____
_____

3 you saw a burglar in your neighbour's house?

_____
_____

4 some friends wanted to go to see an '18' film and you were all only fifteen years old?

_____
_____

Grammar Plus: *If I were you, I'd …*

6 (**) Write advice for each person. Use the verbs below and *If I were you, I'd … .*

> ask her to go out with you   get a Saturday job
> ask your teacher for help   go to the doctor✓

1 'I don't feel well.'

If I were you, I'd go to the doctor.

2 'I really like this girl in my class.'

_____

3 'I don't understand my homework.'

_____

4 'I haven't got any money.'

_____

Grammar reference

Second conditional

Form

We use the second conditional to describe imaginary situations and their results. We use *if* + past simple, and then to talk about the situation we are imagining, we use *would/wouldn't* + verb.

Condition *If* + past simple	Result *would* + infinitive without *to*
If I **was** famous,	I **wouldn't** (= would not) **worry** about studying.
If John **had** a better job,	he'd (= would) **buy** a sports car.
If I **didn't go** to school,	I'd (= would) **stay** in bed until midday.
If you **had** the choice,	**would** you **study** French instead of English?

If can go at the beginning or in the middle of the sentence.

If people didn't pay for music, artists wouldn't make records.
*Artists wouldn't make records **if** people didn't pay for music.*

Sometimes we use *would* on its own, without the *if* clause.

I'd lie about my age.
I wouldn't lie about my age.
***Would** you lie about your age?*
*Yes, I **would**./No, I **wouldn't**.*

> **Notice!**
>
> Compare the meaning of the first and the second conditional sentences.
>
> The first conditional describes a **real** possibility in the future:
> *If I **have** enough money, I'll buy some new shoes on Saturday.*
>
> The second conditional describes an **imaginary** possibility:
> *If I **had** lots of money, I'd buy my own flat.*

Vocabulary

Adjectives ending in -ed and -ing

1 Complete the table with the -ed and -ing form of the adjectives.

Verb	Adjectives
annoy	*annoying/annoyed*
bore	boring/ _____
disappoint	_____ /disappointed
embarrass	embarrassing/ _____
excite	exciting / _____
frighten	_____ /frightened
frustrate	_____ / _____
interest	_____ /interested
please	pleased/ _____
surprise	_____ /surprised
terrify	_____ / _____
worry	_____ / _____

2 Find eight of the adjectives from exercise 1. Look → and ↓.

e	x	c	i	t	i	n	g	w	y
b	q	a	a	w	r	t	t	o	u
o	z	c	v	n	m	g	g	r	b
r	e	x	c	i	t	e	d	r	o
e	a	s	d	f	g	h	m	i	r
d	e	r	r	t	y	i	p	e	i
a	s	f	g	h	j	k	m	d	n
t	e	r	r	i	f	y	i	n	g
a	n	n	o	y	i	n	g	u	o
w	o	r	r	y	i	n	g	t	l

3 Complete the sentences with the correct adjective. There are some extra adjectives.

> annoyed/annoying   frustrated/frustrating
> disappointed/disappointing   bored/boring ✓
> exciting/excited   terrified/terrifying
> worried/worrying

1 I hate football. I think it's really *boring*.
2 Fiona's results were _____ . She usually does very well.
3 Did you see that action film on TV last night? It was great! It was so _____ .
4 Our car broke down in the middle of a forest. It was the most _____ experience of my life.
5 My dad was very _____ when I was caught shoplifting.
6 I just can't understand this exercise at all. It's so _____ .
7 Claudia isn't sleeping well. She is _____ about her exams.

Grammar

Reported requests and commands

4 (*) Match the direct speech in sentences 1–6 to the reported speech in sentences a–f.

1 'Sit down.'
2 'Please, can you sit down?'
3 'Don't sit down.'
4 'Sit down immediately!'
5 'You shouldn't sit down.'
6 'You should sit down.'

a She asked them to sit down.
b She advised them to sit down.
c She told them not to sit down.
d She advised them not to sit down.
e She told them to sit down.
f She ordered them to sit down.

5 (*) Underline the correct words to complete the sentences.

1 'Stop!' the guard said to the shoplifters.
The guard *told/advised* the shoplifters *to stop/stop*.
2 'You should take an aspirin,' Kate said to me.
Kate *ordered/advised* me *to take/take* an aspirin.
3 'Can you pass my book?' Pete's mother said to him.
Pete's mother *asked/told* him to pass *my/her* book.
4 'Put your hands up right now!' the police officer said to the burglar.
The police officer *ordered/advised* the burglar to put *your/his* hands up.
5 'Don't touch the dog!' the mother said to the child.
The mother *told/asked* the child *not to touch/ don't touch* the dog.

6 (**) Complete the sentences in reported speech. Use *tell, order, advise* or *ask*.

1 'Put the baseball bat down,' the police officer said to the burglar.
The police officer *told the burglar to put the baseball bat down*.
2 'Don't be late home,' my father said to me.
My father _____.
3 'Switch your computer off immediately!' Ben's mother said to him.
Ben's mother _____.
4 'You should do more exercise,' the doctor said to Karen.
The doctor _____.
5 'Can you open the window for me?' Rita said to David.
Rita _____.

7 (**) Look at the cartoons. Write the sentences in reported speech.

1   the police officer → the bank robber

   The police officer told the bank robber
   to put his hands in the air.

2   John → his friend

   _____

3   boy → his teacher

   _____

4   teacher → the students

   _____

5   the dentist → the man

   _____

6   the girl → the dog

   _____

8 (***) Read the story and then put the direct speech into reported speech.

One night Julian was coming home late from a party. Suddenly all the lights in the street went off and he couldn't see anything. When he got home, he couldn't open the front door! Julian climbed in a window. He heard a voice. [1] 'Don't move!' a man said. Julian was terrified. [2] 'Lie on the floor,' the man said. [3] 'Please don't hurt me,' Julian said. Suddenly the lights came on again and Julian saw his neighbour with a baseball bat. Julian was in the wrong house! [4] 'You should carry a torch in the future,' his neighbour said. Julian laughed. [5] 'Can you lend me one?' he asked.

1   *A man told Julian not to move.*

2   _____ .

3   _____ .

4   _____ .

5   _____ .

Grammar reference

Reported requests and commands

Direct and reported speech

When we report what someone said we can give the person's exact words (direct speech):

'Go away,' she said to him.
'Please can you pass me the sugar?' I asked her.

Or we can use a verb that describes what they said (reported speech):

*She **told him to go away**.*
*I **asked her to pass** me the sugar.*

Reported requests and commands

We report requests and commands using *ask/tell* + infinitive.

Direct speech	Reported speech
'Hurry up!' I said to my friends.	*I **told** my friends **to hurry** up.*
'Can you help me?' Ann asked him.	*Ann **asked** him **to help** her*

> **Notice!**
> Remember word order in the negative form.
> *'Don't say a word.'* → *He told her **not to say** a word.*

Other reporting verbs

You can use other reporting verbs, for example, *order* or *advise* to show how or why the person spoke.

Direct speech	Reported speech
'Go to bed immediately!'	*She **ordered** the children **to go** to bed immediately.*
'I think you should apologise.'	*He **advised** me **to apologise**.*

> **Notice!**
> These reporting verbs *order* and *advise* take a noun/pronoun (*the children, me*) + infinitive (*to go, to apologise*).
>
> *He **ordered** the children **to go** back to the classroom.*
> *She **advised** me **to apologise** to my friend.*

Vocabulary

Crime

1 Match the verbs in column A with the phrases in column B.

A	B
1 threaten	**a** valuable possessions
2 get	**b** a crime
3 have	**c** someone with violence
4 protect	**d** victim of crime
5 commit	**e** yourself
6 be a	**f** someone for something
7 blame	**g** someone/something
8 fear	**h** hurt

2 Complete the 'word map' with the words below. Then add your own ideas.

> commit ✓   threaten   valuable possessions
> blame   protect   a crime   a victim   fear
> get hurt   commit a crime   violence

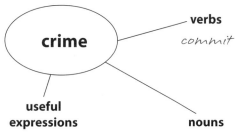

verbs
commit

crime

useful
expressions   nouns

*report a crime
to the police*

3 Use the words below to complete the sentences. You do not need all the words.

> victim   protect   threaten   get hurt
> valuable possessions ✓   fear   commit
> blame

1 Teenagers have more _valuable possessions_ nowadays.

2 If you are the _____ of a crime, you should go to the police as soon as possible.

3 Lots of teenagers give their valuables to robbers because they don't want to _____.

4 Reports want to _____ teenagers for the rise in crime because they carry expensive items with them.

5 It's easier to _____ someone if they are alone so always go out in a group of people.

6 What is your worst _____?

Reading

4 Read the introduction to a novel and choose the correct answers.

The Curious Incident of the Dog in the Night-Time is a murder mystery novel like no other. The detective, and narrator, is Christopher Boone. Christopher is fifteen and has Asperger's Syndrome, a form of autism. He knows a lot about Maths and very little about people. He loves lists, patterns and the truth. He hates the colours yellow and brown and he hates people to touch him. He has never gone further than the end of the road on his own, but when he finds out that someone has killed a neighbour's dog, he starts a terrifying journey that changes his whole world.

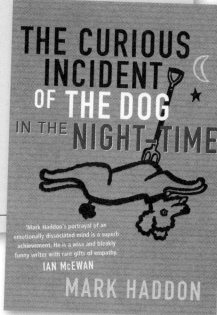

1 *The Curious Incident of the Dog in the Night-Time* is

   a a typical detective story.

   b a book about autistic children.

   c an unusual mystery story.

2 Christopher is good at

   a Maths.

   b telling the truth.

   c understanding people.

3 Christopher … on his own.

   a often explores the town

   b never usually goes to places

   c always goes to other roads

4 When Christopher decides to investigate a crime

   a his life changes a lot.

   b nothing changes in his life.

   c he travels all over the world.

The next day was Saturday and there is not much to do on a Saturday so I decided to do some more detective work on my own.

I decided to go and ask other people who live in our street if they had seen anything strange on Thursday night.

Talking to strangers is not something I usually do. I do not like talking to strangers because I do not like people I have never met before. They are hard to understand. When there is a new teacher at school, I don't talk to them for weeks and weeks. I just watch them until I know they are safe. Then I ask them questions about themselves, like whether they have pets and what is their favourite colour, what kind of car they drive and I ask them to draw a plan of their house so I get to know them.

So talking to other people in our street was brave. But if you are going to do detective work you have to be brave, so I had no choice.

I noticed the old lady who lives at number thirty-nine was in the front garden cutting her hedge. Her name is Mrs Alexander. She has a dog. It is a Dachshund, so she's probably a good person because she likes dogs. But the dog wasn't in the garden with her. It was inside the house.

I went up to Mrs Alexander and said, 'Do you know anything about Wellington*?'

And she said, 'I heard about it yesterday. Dreadful. Dreadful.'

I said, 'Do you know who killed him?'

And she said, 'No, I don't.'

I said, 'Thank you for helping me with my investigation.'

And she said, 'You're Christopher, aren't you?'

I said, 'Yes. I live at number thirty-six.'

And she said, 'It's very nice of you to come and say hello.'

I didn't reply to this because Mrs Alexander was doing what is called chatting where people say things to each other which aren't questions and answers and aren't connected. I was about to turn and walk away when she said, 'I have a grandson your age.'

I tried to do chatting by saying, 'My age is fifteen years and three months and three days.'

And she said, 'Well, almost your age.'

Then she said, 'Do you want to come in for tea?'

And I said, 'I don't go into other people's houses.'

And she said, 'Well, maybe I could bring some out here. Do you like biscuits?'

And I said, 'Yes, some sorts of biscuits.'

Then she turned and went into the house. She moved very slowly because she was an old lady and she was inside the house for more than six minutes and I began to get very nervous because I didn't know what she was doing in the house. I didn't know her well enough to know whether she was telling the truth.

So I walked away.

---

* Wellington is the name of the dog that was killed.

84

---

5 Read a page from the novel and tick (✓) true, cross (✗) false or write (?) if the text doesn't say.

1 ☐ Christopher is usually very busy on Saturday.

2 ☐ Christopher needs time to understand people that he hasn't met before.

3 ☐ Mrs Alexander lives on her own.

4 ☐ Mrs Alexander hasn't heard the news about Wellington.

5 ☐ Mrs Alexander can't give Christopher any information about who killed the dog.

6 ☐ Mrs Alexander's grandson looks very similar to Christopher.

7 ☐ Mrs Alexander goes to make some tea for herself and Christopher to have in the garden.

8 ☐ Christopher leaves because he gets bored.

Reading

Multiple choice

1 Read the first paragraph of a film review and the question. A student has worked with the text to choose the right answer. Tick (✓) the correct answer and cross (✗) the wrong ones.

New on DVD ...

It is not easy to make a traditional detective novel into a film. A lot of what makes it interesting – the thought process of solving the mystery – is difficult to show on screen. This often leads to long scenes in which the detective talks to other characters, explaining his ideas.

Why is it hard to film a detective novel?

a ☐ It's difficult to show the mystery.
It's difficult to show 'the thought process', not the mystery.

b ☐ The characters always talk too much.
The detective (one character) often (not always) talks a lot.

c ☐ Some things are not easy to present visually *'difficult to show on screen'*

2 Read the second paragraph and the question. Choose the correct answer. Use the <u>underlined</u> phrases to help you. Explain why the wrong answers are not correct.

Murder on the Orient Express by Agatha Christie is set in the 1930s. The Orient Express, a luxury train travelling from Istanbul to Calais, is stuck in deep snow somewhere near Belgrade. On board are a <u>Russian</u> princess, a <u>Hungarian</u> diplomat with his beautiful wife, a <u>British</u> army officer, a talkative <u>American</u> widow and a number of other characters, including the famous detective Hercule Poirot. During the night, a man is murdered in his compartment. Poirot <u>is asked by the railway company</u> to solve the mystery. Step by step, he discovers <u>the links between the victim and the remaining twelve passengers</u>. It is certainly one of the best crime novels ever written.

The passengers on the train

a belong to different European nationalities.

b have connections to the murdered man.

c ask Poirot to solve the mystery.

Exam TIP

To eliminate wrong answers, find information in the text which shows why they are wrong.

3 Read the rest of the review and choose the right answers to the questions. <u>Underline</u> the phrases which helped you.

For the 1974 film version director Sydney Lumet brought together a cast of the greatest stars of the day, including Sean Connery, Ingrid Bergman, Michael York and Lauren Bacall. The film is filled with glamorous interiors, beautiful people wearing beautiful clothes, exotic locations and every sort of luxury. (In fact, a real crime was committed during the production when all the expensive food ordered for one of the scenes was stolen!) A real Orient Express engine from the 1930s was borrowed from a museum and filmed on location in the French Alps.

Some viewers thought the film was brilliant. Others found Albert Finney's acting as Poirot unnatural, and the whole movie a bit boring. Agatha Christie preferred it to all other film versions of her novels. So, if you want to have an opinion, see it for yourself!

1 Which reason for the film's success is *not* given in the text?

   a a good script

   b attractive scenery

   c famous actors

2 What were viewers' opinions of the film?

   a Most of them thought it was great.

   b Nearly all of them thought it was boring.

   c Some of them disliked one of the actors.

Use of English

Sentence transformation

Exam **TIP**

Certain pairs of structures often appear in sentence transformation tasks. It is a good idea to learn them.

4 Complete the second sentence so that it means the same as the first. Use no more than three words.

1 Active ↔ passive (attention: different tenses)

The Lumière brothers made the first film in 1895.

The first film _____ the Lumière brothers in 1895.

2 Sentence with *because* ↔ second conditional

I don't buy CDs because they are so expensive.

If CDs weren't so expensive, _____ buy them.

3 Direct speech ↔ reported speech

'You should watch DVDs in English,' the teacher said to Elena.

The teacher advised _____ DVDs in English.

4 Comparisons: *more … than… ↔ not as … as*

Recent films are more violent than old ones.

Old films are not _____ recent ones.

5 Past with *in/on*… (date) or *ago* ↔ present perfect with *since* or *for*

Francis Coppola started working in film in 1960.

Francis Coppola _____ in film since 1960.

5 Complete the second sentence so that it means the same as the first. Use no more than three words.

1 I watch old films because I'm interested in the history of cinema.

If I wasn't interested in the history of cinema, I _____ old films.

2 We came to live here twenty years ago.

We _____ here for twenty years.

3 This comedy was funnier than the one we watched last week.

The comedy we watched last week wasn't _____ this one.

4 'Don't touch anything!' the officer said to us.

The officer ordered _____ touch anything.

5 Our studio has made twenty films this year.

Twenty new films _____ by our studio this year.

Speaking

Guided conversation

6 Read the task and do the preparation exercises below.

Imagine the following situation. You and your friend are going to spend the evening at home watching TV. Here are some pictures of programmes you could watch. Decide together which three programmes you are going to see.

3 _____

4 _____

5 _____

6 _____

1 *sports programme*   2 _____

a Write the names of the types of TV programme under the pictures.

b Complete gaps 1–7 with the words below and gaps a–f with names of TV programmes from exercise 6a.

[great   about   idea   interested interesting   Let's ✓   would]

A: [1] *Let's* watch the [a]_____ .

B: But I'm not really [2]_____ in sports.

A: So what [3]_____ you like to watch?

B: I'd like to see the [b]_____ .

A: Oh, come on! They're for little children.

B: I just like them… We're not going to watch the [c]_____, are we?

A: No, it's not [4]_____ to watch someone cooking food which you can't eat.

B: How [5]_____ the [d]_____? We'll see who can answer the questions faster!

A: Okay. That's a good [6]_____ . But perhaps we should watch the [e]_____ first.

B: Yes, we should know what's happening in the world, shouldn't we?

A: And then part thirty-five of our favourite [f]_____ . We need to know if Lucinda will marry Jeremy, don't we.

B: That sounds [7]_____ .

self-assessment test 6

Vocabulary & Grammar

1 Match an adjective from column A with a noun from column B.

A	B
1 comedy	a programme
2 quiz	b opera
3 soap	c forecast
4 special	d show
5 cookery	e story
6 film	f series
7 short	g effect
8 weather	h studio

/7

2 Complete the sentences with one adjective in each gap. You can see the first letter of each adjective.

1 The film was so b*oring* that we left the cinema.

2 Ann's exam results were really d_____ .
She hoped for about 90 percent but she got only 65 percent.

3 I'm s_____ that Tom wants to invite Gill to his party. He doesn't like her.

4 I forgot the words and stopped singing in the middle of the song. In front of the whole school! It was so e_____ !

5 You should read the article about global warming in yesterday's newspaper. It's very i_____ .

6 I was t_____ when I saw a big black dog following my little sister.

7 Our coach is p_____ with our team. We won the match!

/6

3 Complete the second conditional sentences with the correct form of the verbs in brackets.

1 If I *had* (have) more money, I *would buy* (buy) this CD.

2 What would you do if somebody _____ (threaten) you with a knife?

3 I _____ (not drop) litter if there _____ (be) more rubbish bins in the street.

4 If you _____ (wear) a coat in the winter, you _____ (not get) ill so often.

5 Susan _____ (look) much better if she _____ (not use) so much make-up.

/7

4 Complete the sentences with the verbs below in the correct passive form.

> translate protect blame attack
> download direct ✓ commit

1 *Schindler's List* *was directed* by Steven Spielberg.

2 More and more crimes each year _____ by young people.

3 His book _____ into three languages already.

4 Last week my younger brother _____ in the street.

5 Robbie's parents _____ many times for his bad behaviour at school.

6 Thousands of songs _____ illegally every day.

7 It was very hot at the music festival but we _____ from the sun by the trees.

/6

5 Use the verbs below to report the requests and commands.

> advise ✓ tell ask order advise

1 'Take your driving test later, Lisa.'
(Lisa's best friend → Lisa)
Lisa's best friend advised her to take her driving test later.

2 'Can you help me with my Maths homework?' (I → my older brother)

_____

3 'You should go to the doctor.'
(My father → my mother)

_____

4 'Stop playing football in the classroom!'
(Our teacher → Eddie and Nick)

_____

5 'Don't take my clothes!'
(My older sister → I)

_____

/4

Reading

6 Read the article about a teenage crime survey. Choose the correct answers.

Teenage Crime Survey Published

Children's charity National Children's Homes (NCH) have published the results of a teenage crime study. The study, 'Step Inside Our Shoes: Young People's Views On Gun And Knife Crime', questioned more than 800 young people (all of them under twenty-five) over a six-month period.

Chief executive Clare Tickell said: 'The results of our survey show what young people think of gun and knife crime and any experiences they have had.'

NCH warned that teenagers were worried about crimes in their area and often felt in danger. Some of them know a lot about gun crime or know someone that has been attacked in the street. One in ten young people has been personally affected by gun and knife crime, the report claims.

Young people were asked about the main reasons why other young people started fighting violently on the street. Almost 66 percent of respondents blamed drugs, followed by self-protection (63 percent), image (63 percent) and pressure from school friends (63 percent). Forty-six percent said violent music and computer games could be the main reason for gun and knife crime and 53 percent said sending seventeen to twenty-one-year-olds to prison for a longer time could help reduce such crime.

Ms Tickell said: 'We need to stop thinking of young people as the problem. They can help us find a solution. And we need to find it quickly because our streets are more dangerous than they used to be.'

1 The people who were questioned were

   a people who were twenty-five years old.

   b young people who have been victims of crime.

   c people younger than twenty-five years old.

2 The results of the survey showed that many teenagers

   a were dangerous.   b committed crimes.

   c didn't feel safe.

3 _____ of teenagers have experienced crime in some way.

   a 1 percent   b 10 percent   c 25 percent

4 Almost half of the young people who answered the questions

   a think that teenagers who commit crimes should be sent to prison for a longer time.

   b blame violent music and games for crime among many teenagers.

   c believe that some teenagers commit crimes because of their friends.

5 Ms Tickell thinks that young people

   a can be helpful.   b cause a lot of problems.

   c are more dangerous than before.

/5

Listening

7 (14) Listen to three friends coming out of the cinema. Write the correct names: Sam, Michael, Ellie.

Who:

1 wants to see the film again? _____

2 got frightened several times? _____

3 thinks that cinema tickets are too expensive?

   _____

4 was disappointed with the music?

   _____

5 suggested going somewhere together after the film? _____

6 was a little bored by the story? _____

/6

Communication

8 Put the sentences in the correct order to make dialogues.

1

a ☐ My name's Ian Williams. I'm calling about the football match we're playing tomorrow.

b ☐ Who's calling?

c [1] Hello?

d ☐ Oh, yes, just a minute, I'll get him.

e ☐ Hello, could I speak to David, please?

2

a ☐ Why don't you try her mobile?

b [1] Hello?

c ☐ Oh hi Hannah. No, she isn't here at the moment. Can I take a message?

d ☐ Hi, Becky, it's Hannah, is Claire there?

e ☐ Oh yes, good idea, thanks.

f ☐ Oh don't worry, it's okay.

/9

Marks

Vocabulary & Grammar	/30 marks
Reading	/5 marks
Listening	/6 marks
Communication	/9 marks
Total:	/50 marks

Reading

1 Read the text. Tick (✓) true or cross (✗) false.

Growing up fifty years ago

Julie Haworth from Year 12 interviewed her grandmother about growing up in the 1950s and 1960s in Lancashire and Liverpool. Here is Mrs Haworth's story.

I was born in 1943, during the Second World War. I don't remember the war – I was too little. The first years after the war were quite difficult. We didn't have many things. I always wore my cousin's old dresses. However, compared to the lives of people in Europe, we were very lucky and I was a happy child – I had both parents and two brothers, and the three of us played outdoors all day, so life was good. We didn't have television, but we had a radio and listened to music and to *The Archers*. On 2 June 1953 we went to our neighbours' house to watch the coronation of Queen Elizabeth II. We got our first TV, a small black and white one, much later.

My favourite subject at school was English. I loved reading. I was a good student and I did well in the 11+ exam – an exam everyone took at the age of eleven – so I went to a grammar school, that was a good school that prepared you for university. It was a big thing for a little country girl like me. I learned Latin and French and read a lot of Shakespeare.

After the war, it became possible for students from poorer families to go to university thanks to financial help from the new government. So after my A-levels, I went to Liverpool University to study Literature. That was in 1961. The Beatles were just becoming famous. My friends and I sometimes went to the Cavern to hear them sing. I actually saw John Lennon and Paul McCartney singing maybe ten metres away from me. We had a good time at university – we studied hard, but we also went out and danced a lot. I met my first boyfriend there. As we got older, we became more serious: we were interested in politics and sometimes took part in protests. We went to the theatre a lot. And then, well, I finished university, got my first job with a local newspaper, married my boyfriend, and so, well, I became an adult …

1 ☐ As a child Julie's grandmother didn't have many new clothes.
2 ☐ Mrs Haworth's childhood was sad.
3 ☐ As a child Mrs Haworth never watched TV.
4 ☐ Mrs Haworth went to grammar school because of good exam results.
5 ☐ Mrs Haworth could go to university because her parents had money.
6 ☐ At university, Mrs Haworth and her friends were only interested in pop music.

/6

Listening

2 (15) A teacher is talking to parents about a planned school trip. Listen to the recording twice and complete the missing information.

School trip to the Lake District

Leaving on Thursday, the 14th of [1]_____
Returning on Sunday the 17th
Staying in youth hostel in [2]_____
Leaving at exactly [3]_____
Students should bring [4]_____ walking shoes.
Maximum pocket money: [5]_____
Please fill in yellow forms with emergency [6]_____ details.

/6

Use of English

3 Choose the correct answer a, b or c to complete the text.

The more the merrier?

Peter is an [1] *b* child and he enjoys it. He likes [2] ___ alone. He [3] ___ a lot and plays the guitar. When he wants to be with people, he [4] ___ out with his friends. Because he has no brothers or sisters, his parents have more time and more money just [5] ___ him.

Peter's girlfriend Marianne has three brothers and two sisters. She loves it. There's never a boring moment in their house. [6] ___the evenings they all have dinner together and talk about their day. Sometimes they [7] ___ instruments. Last Christmas they [8] ___ a concert for their family and friends.

In the future Marianne would like [9] ___ a lot of children, [10] ___ Peter thinks one is enough. Of course, they still have a lot of time to decide, but they are planning to get engaged soon.

1	**a** single	**b** only	**c** one
2	**a** being	**b** to be	**c** be
3	**a** read	**b** reading	**c** reads
4	**a** meets	**b** goes	**c** gets
5	**a** on	**b** to	**c** for
6	**a** In	**b** On	**c** At
7	**a** playing	**b** play	**c** to play
8	**a** give	**b** giving	**c** gave
9	**a** having	**b** have	**c** to have
10	**a** so	**b** but	**c** if

/9

4 Complete the text with the words below. There are two extra words.

> afford   because   go   going   for   forms
> is   long   passed   was   when   while✓

A dream come true

[1]*While* I was at university I worked part-time as a waiter and I even saved some money. My plan was to travel around Europe after finishing my studies. But I also needed a job, and as soon as I [2] ___ my final exams I started looking [3] ___ one. I read adverts, filled in application [4] ___ and went for interviews. Nobody offered me a job, [5] ___ I had no experience in a big company. Then I used my 'travel money' to start my own small business. I worked very [6]___ hours and had no holiday for two years. My mother [7] ___ worried and she often asked: '[8] ___ are you going on holiday, dear?' I couldn't leave my work then, but now I can – and I can [9] ___ a trip around Europe. In fact, I'm [10] ___ to Barcelona tomorrow. It will be wonderful to go sightseeing and not sit at my desk.

/9

Marks

Reading	/6 marks
Listening	/6 marks
Use of English	/18 marks
Total:	/30 marks

Reading

1 Read the descriptions below. Choose the best sports club A–E for each person 1–4. There is one extra club.

1 ☐ Chris is twenty-two and he's a university student. He is fit and sporty and enjoys fast games. He's good at football and basketball and now he'd like to try another team game. He's got a lot of time, but not very much money.

2 ☐ Patrick is a forty-year-old writer. He spends whole days working in his study. He is unfit and a bit lonely. He would like to take up an outdoor activity and meet some people. He hasn't got fixed working hours. He's allergic to animals.

3 ☐ Christine is thirty and works for a large company. After a day in the office, she is tired of people and technology. She'd like to learn an outdoor activity that she can do alone in nice scenery. She hasn't got a car.

4 ☐ Paul and Natalie are eighteen. They met through their school's basketball team. Now they'd like to take up a game they can play together in the evenings and at weekends. They don't want to buy any equipment until they are sure they like the sport.

A Concorde Squash Club

The courts, conveniently located in the centre of town, are open seven days a week from 10 a.m. to 9 p.m. Weekday and weekend lessons available for both beginners and advanced players. You will need shorts and trainers; rackets and balls can be hired for an extra fee.

Northumbrian Rock Climbing Club

B Looking for a new challenge? Try an exciting activity and discover the unique friendship between people who climb together. Rock-climbing courses start every month. We accept beginners, but you need to be reasonably fit. A twenty minute drive from the city centre – see the map for details.

C Luneside Riding Club

You can begin horse riding at any age. After you've completed a basic fifty hour course (both individual and group lessons available), you are free to take rides across fields and forests, alone or with other club members. Only forty minutes by train from the city centre.

D Morecambe Sailing and Watersports Centre

You can start sailing at any age and you do not have to be very fit. Two week full-time courses for beginners start every two weeks. Learn the basics of sailing, meet new people, discover the fun and companionship of being part of a team …, and start exploring England's beautiful lakes and rivers with your new friends.

E Academic Ice Hockey Club

Next ice hockey course for beginners starts on October 30. Men's and women's teams separate. Practice two afternoons a week, friendly matches at weekends. You will need your own skates; all other equipment can be hired. Discounts for holders of the International Student Identity Card.

/4

Listening

2 (16) You are going to hear a tour guide talking to a group of tourists in Hampton Court Palace. Listen to the recording twice and choose the right answer.

1 The group are now going to
   a visit King Henry the Eighth's apartments.
   b have some time to themselves.
   c have a guided tour of the whole palace.

2 In the kitchens, staff prepared food
   a for over two hundred people.
   b three times a day.
   c for more than a thousand people.

3 You can get an audio guide from
   a the information centre.
   b the coffee shop.
   c the palace gardens.

4 The guide recommends
   a the gardens.
   b the cafés.
   c King William's and Queen Mary's rooms.

5 For those who are hungry, the guide suggests
   a two different places.
   b the restaurant next to the kitchens.
   c the restaurant at the hotel.

6 The group are going to have dinner
   a at 5.30.   b at 6.30.   c at 8.00.

/6

Use of English

3 Complete the gaps with the correct form of the words in brackets.

I had a very happy [1] _childhood_ (child). We lived in the countryside and we played outside all the time. We had a lot of [2] _____ (free). My brother and I sometimes had [3] _____ (argue) but most of the time we got on very well. We both had [4] _____ (responsible) at home: we had to clean our rooms and do the [5] _____ (wash-) up. Sometimes we got an [6] _____ (invite) to our neighbours'. They had a huge, [7] _____ (amaze) garden and we loved playing there. Now my family and I live in the city, but we spend our weekends and holidays in the country. We go [8] _____ (cycle) and play games. I think children need to be [9] _____ (act). It's very [10] _____ (health) for them to be indoors in front of the TV all the time. Most kids prefer to do something more [11] _____ (excite) if they can.

/10

4 Put the words in the correct order to make sentences. The first word is given.

1 Europe/travelled/never/outside/I/have
   I _____
   _____ .

2 orange/can/glass/have/a/juice/I/large/of
   Can _____
   _____ ?

3 hanging/friends/out/David/the/with/evening/in/enjoys
   David _____
   _____ .

4 prize/she/competition/in/ever/a/has/a/won
   Has _____
   _____ ?

5 go/the/you/usually/holiday/on/where/in/do/summer
   Where _____
   _____ ?

6 this/finish/we/week/definitely/next/project/will
   We _____
   _____ .

7 expensive/bike/a/more/car/than/is/a
   A _____
   _____ .

8 might/and/afternoon/in/sightseeing/the/Lucy/I/go
   Lucy _____
   _____ .

9 phoned /my/was/I/my/homework/while/friend/doing
   My _____
   _____ .

10 TV/allowed/not/after/are/children/to/their/watch/8 p.m.
   Their _____
   _____ .

/10

Marks
Reading	/4 marks
Listening	/6 marks
Use of English	/20 marks
Total:	/30 marks

exam test 2

113

exam test 3

Reading

1 Read the film review and choose the correct answer to the questions.

Dante's Peak, 1997 (director Roger Donaldson)
Saturday at 19.00 on MovieTime Channel

On a lovely summer day, the small town of Dante's Peak in the Cascade Mountains is celebrating. It has just received an award for being the second best place to live in the USA. Nobody is thinking of the nearby volcano, which hasn't been active for years.

The scientist Dr Harry Dalton (played by Pierce Brosnan) is sent to Dante's Peak to study the volcano. He finds dead plants and animals. He thinks the mountain is not a safe place to be for people, and he tries to get the local council to prepare an evacuation. But nobody listens to him. They are afraid businesspeople will not invest in the town if they think it is a dangerous place. Even Dalton's boss, Dr Paul Dreyfuss, is against him. The only person who believes him is the mayor of the town, Rachel Wando (Linda Hamilton), a single mother of two children.

Soon, the mountain begins to cause serious problems and the people in the town realise the big danger of the volcano. But it's too late. The volcano erupts. Day becomes night; air turns to fire; buildings fall; people panic as they run for their lives through the ash and dust. Harry and Rachel discover that Rachel's children have gone up the mountain to try and save their grandmother. They follow them. Fighting against the volcano, Harry, Rachel, and the children are the only people left in the destroyed town, and that's not the end – the second eruption is still to come.

If you've seen one disaster movie, you've seen them all. You can guess who will die and who will live and of course who will fall in love. But the action is fast and the special effects are still fun to watch after ten years. Okay, if you look carefully, you can see that the cars on the falling bridge are models with no drivers inside. But you'd never know the volcanic ash is really little bits of newspaper! The ground shakes, red hot rocks come down from the sky, and there are lots of deep low sound effects. A good way to spend a Saturday evening.

1 At the beginning of the movie, people in Dante's Peak are
- **a** surprised by the good weather.
- **b** afraid of the volcano.
- **c** happy because they've won a prize.
- **d** very active.

2 The people in the town don't listen to Dr Dalton because
- **a** the volcano is not active.
- **b** a dangerous volcano would be bad for business.
- **c** his boss doesn't agree with him.
- **d** they are enjoying the party.

3 Rachel's children are not at home because
- **a** they've gone to play with their grandmother.
- **b** they've gone out to look at the mountain.
- **c** they have run away in panic.
- **d** they are trying to save someone.

4 After Rachel and Harry find the children
- **a** there is a happy ending.
- **b** the town is destroyed.
- **c** they have to face more danger.
- **d** day becomes night.

5 The writer thinks the story is
- **a** boring and not much fun.
- **b** easy to predict but entertaining.
- **c** very romantic but not fun to watch.
- **d** terrifying but fun to watch.

6 On the whole, what is the writer's opinion of the film?
- **a** He thinks the special effects are all old and boring.
- **b** He likes the sound effects best.
- **c** He would like it better if the heroes didn't fall in love.
- **d** He recommends it as weekend entertainment.

/6

Listening

2 (17) Read statements 1–6. Then listen twice to a man reporting a crime. Tick (✓) true or cross (✗) false.

1 ☐ Mark is not from the town where the crime happened.
2 ☐ The attackers threatened Mark with violence.
3 ☐ Mark can describe the robbers well.
4 ☐ Mark is interested in football.
5 ☐ Mark doesn't know how much some of his possessions cost.
6 ☐ Mark is too frightened to return home alone.

/6

Use of English

3 Complete the second sentence so that it means the same as the first. Use one to three words.

1 I found the news surprising.
I was _surprised by_ the news.

2 The doctor said to Tom, 'You should eat more fruit.'
The doctor advised _____ more fruit .

3 The teacher asked Mike to prepare a presentation.
Mike _____ the teacher to prepare a presentation.

4 Matt's car is faster than Jeremy's.
Jeremy's car is not _____ Matt's.

5 It last rained a month ago.
It _____ for a month.

6 'Could you please move your car?' the police officer said to Mary.
The police officer asked _____ her car.

7 You don't get good results because you don't study hard.
If you _____, you would get good results.

8 They have opened a new club in our area.
A new club _____ in our area.

9 Kitty thought the film was disappointing.
Kitty was _____ the film.

10 The guide said to the tourists, 'Don't make a noise!'
The guide told the tourists _____ a noise.

/9

4 Complete the text with one word in each gap.

Dove Cottage

Grasmere is [1] _a_ little village in the Lake District, in the north of England. [2] _____ you go there, don't forget to visit Dove Cottage, the charming little house [3] _____ the poet William Wordsworth lived in the 19th century with [4] _____ sister, Dorothy. William wrote poems and Dorothy wrote a diary [5] _____ tells us a lot about their life. It was much slower and more peaceful [6] _____ life in the 21st century. William and Dorothy used [7] _____ go for long walks around the lakes and write long letters to their friends. While William [8] _____ writing, Dorothy worked in the garden. They [9] _____ regularly visited by their friend, the poet Samuel Taylor Coleridge. Today, the cottage is [10] _____ museum and Dorothy's garden is as beautiful as it was when she looked after it.

/9

Marks
Reading   /6 marks
Listening   /6 marks
Use of English /18 marks
Total: /30 marks

exam topic wordlist

people

emotions and feelings
admire (v)
amazed (adj)
angry (adj)
annoyed (adj)
believe in (v)
be tired of (v)
bored (adj)
depressed (adj)
disappointed (adj)
embarrassed (adj)
excited (adj)
fear (v)
frightened (adj)
frustrated (adj)
happy (adj)
impress (v)
interested (adj)
nervous (adj)
pleased (adj)
sad (adj)
scream (v)
shake with fear (v)
surprise (v)
surprised (adj)
terrified (adj)
upset (adj)(v)
worried (adj)
worry (v)

personal qualities
brave (adj)
brilliant (adj)
brutal (adj)
calm (adj)
crazy (adj)
creative (adj)
determined (adj)
easy-going (adj)
energetic (adj)
fitness freak (n)
friendly (adj)

funny (adj)
generous (adj)
glamorous (adj)
honest (adj)
inspire (v)
intelligent (adj)
kind (adj)
lazy (adj)
mean (adj)
out-of-control (adj)
quiet (adj)
rude (adj)
saver (n)
sense of humour (n)
sensible with money (adj)
spender (n)
strict (adj)
stylish (adj)
sympathetic (adj)
talented (adj)

appearance
beautiful (adj)
dyed hair (n)
glamorous (adj)
jewellery (n)
lipstick (n)
long hair (n)
make-up (n)
piercings (n)
tattoo (n)

clothes
baggy (adj)
business suit (n)
casual (adj)
designer clothes (n)
fashion (n)
jeans (n)
sandals (n)
short trousers (n)
smart (adj)
tight (adj)

unique (adj)
unusual (adj)
wear (v)
well-dressed (adj)
winter coat (n)

personal data
date of birth (n)
email address (n)
emergency contact details (n)
full name (n)
home address (n)
mobile number (n)
nationality (n)
passport number (n)
postcode (n)
UK address (n)

house

in the house
air-conditioning (n)
armchair (n)
chair (n)
coffee table (n)
cupboard (n)
cushion (n)
double bed (n)
mirror (n)
picture (n)
plant (n)
poster (n)
rug (n)
sofa (n)
stool (n)
table (n)
twin-bedded (adj)
wall (n)
wardrobe (n)

describing a house
bright (adj)
colourful (adj)

comfortable (adj)
dark (adj)
messy (adj)
modern (adj)
noisy (adj)
quiet (adj)
stylish (adj)
tidy (adj)
well-organised (adj)

housework
cleaning (n)
do the cooking (v)
do the hoovering (v)
do the ironing (v)
do the washing-up (v)
housework (n)
make a mess (v)
make the beds (v)
tidy (your room) (v)

school

places to study
college (n)
high school (n)
mixed school (n)
nursery (n)
primary school (n)
private school (n)
secondary school (n)
single-sex school (n)
state school (n)
university (n)

subjects
Accountancy (n)
Art (n)
Business studies (n)
Car mechanics (n)
Cookery (n)
Design studies (n)
Drama (n)
DT (Design and Technology) (n)
English language (n)
English literature (n)
European History (n)

Film studies (n)
foreign language (n)
History (n)
ICT (Information and Computer Technology) (n)
Italian (n)
Latin (n)
Law (n)
Management studies (n)
Maths (n)
Media studies (n)
Medicine (n)
Metalwork (n)
Politics (n)
Psychology (n)
Science (n)
Woodwork (n)

people and places
cafeteria (n)
gym (n)
library (n)
overseas student (n)
pupil (n)
school children (n)
student (n)
teacher (n)

learning and exams
A-level (n)
behave well (v)
be terrible at (v)
cheat (v)
compulsory (adj)
concentrate (v)
copy (an essay) (v)
discipline (n & v)
do a course (v)
do badly at school (v)
do homework (v)
drop (a subject) (v)
drop out of school (v)
educate (v)
enrolment form (n)
essay (n)
exam pressures (n)
gap year (n)
GCSE (n)

get a degree (v)
get into trouble (v)
give lessons (v)
go wrong (v)
hand (an essay) in (v)
leave school (v)
miss lessons (v)
not take any notice (v)
pass your exams (v)
play-time (n)
play truant (v)
school project (n)
school uniform (n)
schoolwork (n)
start school (v)
study (v)
summer course (n)
take an exam (v)
teach (v)
test (v)

work

jobs
accountant (n)
actor (n)
au pair (n)
babysit (v)
ballet dancer (n)
businessman (n)
composer (n)
counsellor (n)
deliver newspapers (v)
dentist (n)
doctor (n)
electrician (n)
engineer (n)
farmer (n)
footballer (n)
graphic designer (n)
IT consultant (n)
journalist (n)
lawyer (n)
model (n)
musician (n)
nanny (n)
nurse (n)

pharmacist (n)
pilot (n)
police officer (n)
presenter (n)
producer (n)
receptionist (n)
retired (adj)
sales representative (n)
scientist (n)
social worker (n)
volunteer (n)
writer (n)

looking for a job
advert for vacancies (n)
fill in an application form (v)
get a job (v)
have experience (v)
interview (n)
job hunter (n)
offer a job (v)
qualification (n)
school leaver (n)
start work (v)
unemployment (n)
vacancy (n)
write a CV (v)

money
badly paid (adj)
borrow (v)
earn money (v)
lend (v)
low income (n)
owe (v)
pay someone back (v)
poor (adj)
put money in the bank (v)
rich (adj)
salary (n)
save (v)
wage (n)
well-paid (adj)

describing jobs and skills
career (n)
creative (adj)

glamorous (adj)
good with numbers (adj)
good with people (adj)
good with your hands (adj)
part-time job (n)
rewarding (adj)
secure (adj)
stressful (adj)
successful (adj)
temporary job (n)
work abroad (v)
work indoors/outdoors (v)
work with children/animals/
computers (v)

in the office
businessman (n)
business plan (n)
desk (n)
do the photocopying (v)
employer (n)
file (n)
fly/travel on business (v)
meeting (n)
office (n)
report (n)
sit in front of a computer (v)
staff (n)
start your own company (v)

family and social life

family and life stages
aunt (n)
childhood (n)
cousin (n)
daughter (n)
daughter-in-law (n)
ex-husband (n)
ex-wife (n)
family (n)
father (n)
funeral (n)
generation (n)
grandparent (n)
great-grandfather (n)

great-grandmother (n)
grow up (v)
male (n)
mother (n)
nephew (n)
niece (n)
old (adj)
only child (n)
over-50s (n)
parent (n)
pregnant (adj)
relation (n)
relative (n)
single parent (n)
son (n)
son-in-law (n)
stepfather (n)
stepmother (n)
teenager (n)
twins (n)
uncle (n)
younger/older brother (n)
younger/older sister (n)

relationships
bad influence (n)
become friends (v)
best friend (n)
boyfriend (n)
bring (children) up (v)
close friends (n)
date (n)
divorced (adj)
dump someone (v)
fall in love (v)
forgive (v)
get engaged (v)
get married (v)
get to know (v)
give advice (v)
hang out with somebody (v)
have an argument (v)
keep away from (v)
keep in touch (v)
live happily ever after (v)
look after (v)
(not) get on with someone (v)
relationship (n)

socialise (v)

start going out with someone (v)

support (v)

understand each other (v)

daily routine

bedtime (n)

do nothing (v)

fall asleep (v)

get up (late) (v)

go to bed (early) (v)

go to sleep (v)

habit (n)

have a shower (v)

have an appointment (v)

have some good news (v)

lunchtime (n)

leisure time

birthday party (n)

camping (n)

chess (n)

do sport (v)

enjoy yourself (v)

fancy dress party (n)

farewell party (n)

give presents (v)

go out (v)

go shopping/running/on the computer (v)

go to clubs (v)

go to the cinema/beach (v)

have a party (v)

late-night shopping (n)

leisure activity (n)

make arrangements (n)

make plans (v)

meet new people (v)

meet your friends (v)

nightclub (n)

play a musical instrument (v)

play cards (v)

play computer games (v)

play the drums/guitar (v)

raise money (v)

relaxing (adj)

special occasion (n)

spend time (v)

stay in (v)

stay out late (v)

watch DVDs/a movie (v)

food

food items

bacon (n)

baked potato (n)

banana (n)

bar (of chocolate) (n)

beer (n)

biscuit (n)

bottle (of mineral water) (n)

bowl (of pasta) (n)

box (of pastries) (n)

cabbage (n)

cake (n)

can (of lemonade) (n)

carton (of yoghurt) (n)

cereal (n)

cheese (n)

chicken (n)

coffee (n)

cornflakes (n)

cream (n)

cream cake (n)

curry (n)

dairy products (n)

egg (n)

fish (n)

fish and chips (n)

fizzy drink (n)

fresh fruit (n)

fruit juice (n)

glass (of milk) (n)

grape (n)

ham (n)

hot chocolate (n)

ice-cream (n)

lemon (n)

lemonade (n)

lettuce (n)

loaf (of bread) (n)

margarine (n)

marmalade (n)

meat (n)

milk (n)

milkshake (n)

olive oil (n)

onions (n)

orange (n)

orange juice (n)

packet (of biscuits) (n)

pasta (n)

pepper (n)

piece (of cheese) (n)

pizza (n)

plate (of salad) (n)

potato (n)

salt (n)

sandwich (n)

sausages (n)

soft drink (n)

soup (n)

steak (n)

strawberry (n)

sugar (n)

sweet pastry (n)

sweets (n)

tea (n)

toast (n)

tomato (n)

tuna (n)

vegetable (n)

yoghurt (n)

meals

dinner (n)

elevenses (n)

fill (you) up (v)

have breakfast (v)

have lunch (v)

healthy snack (n)

hot meal (n)

national dish (n)

nibbles (n)

packed lunch (n)

picnic (n)

ready meal (n)

school lunch (n)

snack (n)

takeaway (n)

tea (n)

traditional breakfast (n)

in the kitchen

cooker (n)

dish (n)

dishwasher (n)

do the cooking (v)

fridge (n)

ingredients (n)

make a sandwich (v)

make breakfast (v)

describing food and drink

delicious (adj)

disgusting (adj)

low fat (adj)

starving (adj)

tasty (adj)

thirsty (adj)

shopping and services

types of shops

café (n)

clothes shop (n)

coffee bar (n)

corner shop (n)

drycleaner (n)

grocery store (n)

high street (n)

manufacturer (n)

stationer (n)

supermarket (n)

in a shop

bag (n)

bargain (n)

buy (v)

customer (n)

enter PIN number (v)

fitting room (n)

manager (n)

product (n)

queue (v)

sale (n)

sell (v)

shop assistant (n)

shopkeeper (n)

shopping trip (n)

small/medium/large size (n)

try something on (v)

money

can't afford (v)

change (n)

cheap (adj)

credit card (n)

expensive (adj)

hire (v)

insurance (n)

invest (v)

pay (v)

pocket money (n)

spend (v)

spend a fortune on (v)

complaining

compensation (n)

complain (v)

complaint (n)

exchange (v)

receipt (n)

refund (n)

replacement (n)

scratched (adj)

stain (n)

travelling and tourism

the airport

airline (n)

airport (n)

arrivals gate (n)

board a plane (v)

boarding card (n)

check-in desk (n)

check in your luggage (v)

collect your luggage (v)

delayed (adj)

departure gate (n)

departures board (n)

duty-free shop (n)

fasten seat belt (v)

flight (n)

get off (the plane) (v)

go through passport control (v)

go through security (v)

hand luggage (n)

in-flight movie (n)

land (v)

lose your luggage (v)

one-way ticket (n)

take off (v)

means of transport

bus (n)

coach (n)

railway station (n)

sail (v)

scooter (n)

ship (n)

sports car (n)

train station (n)

travel by coach/plane/train (v)

problems and accidents

accident (n)

car crash (n)

food poisoning (n)

get sunburnt (v)

traffic (n)

traffic jams (n)

holidays

accommodation (n)

beach (n)

book a holiday (v)

brochure (n)

destination (n)

guidebook (n)

holidaymaker (n)

hostel (n)

journey (n)

luggage (n)

luxury hotel (n)

map (n)

market (n)

nature reserve (n)

park (n)

passenger (n)

resort (n)

tent (n)

ticket (n)
tourist (n)
tour operator (n)
travel agent (n)
twin-bedded room (n)

holiday activities
boat trip (n)
camping (n)
eat out (v)
excursion (n)
get sunburnt/food poisoning (v)
go clubbing (v)
go for a walk (v)
go to the beach (v)
guided tour (n)
hang out with friends (v)
have fun (v)
look at scenery (v)
nightlife (n)
paragliding (n)
relaxing (adj)
shopping (n)
sightseeing (n)
sunbathing (n)
swimming (n)
theme park (n)
visit museums and galleries (v)
weekend break (n)
windsurfing (n)

describing holiday locations
amazing (adj)
awful (adj)
boring (adj)
charming (adj)
cool (adj)
exciting (adj)
famous (adj)
fantastic (adj)
historic (adj)
interesting (adj)
lively (adj)
peaceful (adj)
pretty (adj)
special (adj)
stress-free (adj)
unforgettable (adj)

wonderful (adj)
world-famous (adj)

culture
music
band (n)
composer (n)
hit (n)
live band (n)
musician (n)
performance (n)
pop star (n)
rock band (n)
rock concert (n)
singer (n)
single (n)
song (n)
songwriter (n)

film
actors (n)
an 18 film (n)
budget (n)
cinema (n)
designer (n)
dialogue (n)
director (n)
dub (v)
dubbing (n)
editing (n)
fantasy/science fiction (n)
(film) on location (v)
film studios (n)
foreign-language film (n)
historical drama (n)
horror movie (n)
narrator (n)
producer (n)
publicity (n)
release (a film) (v)
romantic comedy (n)
scene (n)
script (n)
special effects (n)
star (v)
subtitle (n)
thriller (n)

tv and radio
advert (n)
broadcast (n)
cartoon (n)
character (n)
comedy series (n)
cookery programme (n)
documentary (n)
episode (n)
news (n)
phone-in (n)
quiz show (n)
realistic (adj)
reality show (n)
science fiction drama (n)
soap opera (n)
sports programme (n)
television series (n)
the media (n)
TV channel (n)
TV company (n)
TV presenter (n)
TV programme (n)
version (n)
viewer (n)
weather forecast (n)

things to read
article (n)
comic (n)
diary (n)
diary (n)
internet postings (n)
newspaper (n)
novel (n)
play (n)
poetry (n)
short stories (n)
weblog/blog (n)

art
achieve (v)
artist (n)
create (v)
inspiration (n)
inspire (v)
painting (n)
statue (n)

people

actor (n)
actress (n)
famous (adj)
icon (n)
legend (n) (person)
model (n)
star (n) (person)
viewer (n)

sport

types of sport

badminton (n)
baseball (n)
basketball (n)
boxing (n)
climb (v)
cricket (n)
cycling (n)
fishing (n)
football (n)
golf (n)
go to the gym (v)
hockey (n)
horse riding (n)
paragliding (n)
skiing (n)
surf (v)
table tennis (n)
tennis (n)
volleyball (n)
water sports (n)
windsurfing (n)
yoga (n)

sports people

athlete (n)
ballet dancer (n)
captain (n)
champion (n)
disabled athlete (n)
fan (n)
fitness expert (n)
footballer (n)
national hero (n)
opponent (n)

player (n)
sponsor (n)
sporting hero (n)
sports person (n)
swimmer (n)
substitute (n)
sumo wrestler (n)
team (n)
tennis player (n)
world champion (n)

equipment and places

ball (n)
baseball bat (n)
bicycle (n)
boots (n)
gloves (n)
goggles (n)
ice rink (n)
net (n)
racket (n)
shorts (n)
skates (n)
stick (n)
trainers (n)

sports events

award (v)
beat (someone) (v)
compete internationally (v)
Congratulations! (n)
gold medal (n)
match (n)
play for (England) (v)
prize (n)
represent (a country) (v)
score points (v)
tournament (n)
winner (n)
win races (v)

training

after-school sports club (n)
fitness (n)
fitness programme (n)
indoor/outdoor game (n)
long distance (n)

make progress (v)
speed (n)
strength (n)
throw (v)
train hard (v)
unfit (adj)
warm up (v)

describing sport

exciting (adj)
fantastic (adj)
fast (adj)
good fun (adj)
popular (adj)

health

parts of the body

body (n)
brain (n)
digestion (n)
face (n)
hair (n)
heart (n)
height (n)
knee (n)
skin (n)
teeth (n)
waistline (n)

illness and injury

break an arm/a leg (v)
food poisoning (n)
hospital (n)
ill (adj)
injury (n)
malaria (n)
Parkinson's disease (n)
sick (adj)
suffer from/have depression (v)

healthy and unhealthy lifestyles

drink alcohol (v)
energy (n)
exercise (n)
fat (adj)

fit (adj)
healthy diet (n)
lose weight (v)
put on weight (v)
slim (adj)
smoke (v)
unfit (adj)
use drugs (v)
weak (adj)
weigh (v)

science and technology

science
develop (a theory) (v)
discover (v)
invent (v)
law of gravity (n)
theory of Evolution (n)

computers
click (v)
email address (n)
go online (v)
Internet access (n)
Internet posting (n)
Internet survey (n)
laptop (n)
log on (v)
printer (n)
website/site (n)
wire (n)

technology
alarm clock (n)
answering machine (n)
battery (n)
camcorder (n)
charger (n)
dishwasher (n)
digital camera (n)
flat screen TV (n)
gadget (n)
games console (n)
hairdryer (n)
headphones (n)

instruction book (n)
machine (n)
mobile phone (n)
MP3 player (n)
photocopier (n)
remote control (n)
screen (n)
TV set (n)
volume (n)

useful verbs
break down (v)
charge (the battery) (v)
make a phone call (v)
operate (a machine) (v)
plug (it) in (v)
press a button (v)
put (batteries) in (v)
record messages (v)
select from a menu (v)
set the time (v)
switch (it) on/off (v)
text (v)
turn (the volume) up/down (v)

the environment

landscape
beach (n)
coast (n)
continent (n)
desert (n)
field (n)
forest (n)
island (n)
jungle (n)
lake (n)
moon (n)
mountain range (n)
ocean/sea (n)
river (n)
rock (n)
seashore/shore (n)
the Earth (n)
volcano (n)
waves (n)

animals
alligator (n)
bird (n)
crocodile (n)
duck (n)
elephant (n)
fish (n)
horse (n)
mosquito (n)
penguin (n)
polar bear (n)
rhinoceros (n)
wildlife (n)

environmental issues
climate refugee (n)
crash (v) (waves)
damage the environment (v)
destroy (v)
droughts (n)
explosion (n)
extinct (adj)
extreme weather (n)
farm (v)
floods (n)
global warming (n)
help the environment (v)
high temperatures (n)
hurricane (n)
loud noise (n)
melting ice (n)
nature (n)
pollution (n)
rising sea level (n)
smoke (n)
species (n)
tsunami (n)
volcanic eruption (n)

weather
cold (adj)
cool (adj)
dry (adj)
freeze (v)
frost (n)
frozen (adj)
hot (adj)
rain (v)

snow (v)
sunny (adj)
weather (n)

country and society

crime
attack somebody (v)
(bank) robber (n)
break into (a house) (v)
burglar (n)
burglary (n)
burgle (v)
commit a crime/murder (v)
criminal (n)
download music illegally (v)
drop litter (v)
guilty (adj)
honest (adj)
illegal (adj)
lie (v)
rob (v)
robbery (n)
shoot (v)
shoplifting (n)
speeding (n)
stab (v)
steal (v)
threaten (v)
use fake ID (v)
vandalism (n)
victim (n)
violence (n)
violent (adj)

punishment
age of criminal responsibility (n)
arrest (v)
blame (v)
catch (a criminal) (v)
control (v)
death penalty (n)
discipline (v)
execute (v)
go to prison (v)
judge (v & n)
punish (v)

war
atomic bomb (n)
battle (n)
gunfire (n)
join the army (v)
lead (an army) (v)
military leader (n)
peace (n)
refuse to fight (v)

society
ban (v)
be banned (v)
break the rules (v)
driver's licence (n)
fear (v)
freedom (n)
get hurt (v)
guide (v)
ID (n)
law (n)
pensioner (n)
protect (v)
republic (n)
retired (adj)
rights (n)
take a driving test (v)
voluntary service (n)
vote (v)

people
chairman (n)
counsellor (n)
king (n)
Member of Parliament (n)
parliament (n)
political leader (n)
political party (n)
president (n)
presidential candidate (n)
Prime Minister (n)
queen (n)
royalty (n)
spokesman (n)

information about English speaking countries

places
the UK
Big Ben (n)
Britain (n)
Buckingham Palace (n)
Central London (n)
Heathrow Airport (n)
London (n)
Piccadilly Circus (n)
River Thames (n)
Scotland (n)
Tower of London (n)
Trafalgar Square (n)

the USA
Arizona Desert (n)
Brat Camp (n)
California (n)
Disney World (theme park) (n)
Everglades Nature Reserve/
National Park (in Florida) (n)
Florida (n)
Hollywood (n)
New York (n)
Ohio (n)
Orlando (n)
Yale University (n)

events
Commonwealth Games (n)
Football World Cup (n)
London Marathon (n)
Second World War (n)
Winter Olympics (n)
World University Games (n)

functions list

Greeting, meeting and getting to know people

Meeting and greeting
How do you do?
Nice to meet you.
Great to see you again!
Let me introduce you.
This is my brother, Ted.
Welcome to London!
Thanks, it's great to be here!
How was your journey?

Getting to know people
What's your nationality?
Where are you from?
What's your full name?
Which part of (Poland) are you from?
Which course are you doing?
How about you?
Where are you staying?
Are you enjoying London?
What's your date of birth?
Do you like London/this music?
What's your favourite CD ever?
How do you spend Sundays?
What kind of music/books do you like/read?
Which city do you come from originally?
How many brothers and sisters have you got?
Do you get on well with your brother/sister?

Narrating past events

Time expressions
after a few months
when he was fourteen
In 1985
after that
then
after a couple of years

Describing how you felt
It was terrible/amazing/incredible!
I was terrified/frightened/scared!
I still can't believe it!

Responding with interest
That's amazing/incredible!
Wow!
Really?
Oh, no!

Talking about famous people

He/She was a brilliant (artist).
He was the best (footballer) in the world.
She/He wrote/composed/invented/discovered …
He/She was the greatest (scientist) in our history.
She/He was the first person to …
He/She won …
He led the country when …
My sporting hero is …
She was born in …
She started running when she was twelve.
Her early career was very successful.
He won three gold medals.
She has inspired a lot of young people.
I like him because he's very determined.

Describing a picture

In the centre/middle of the room …
On the right/left of the picture, there is/are …
On the floor/wall/table there is/are …
Behind/near/next to the sofa …
There is/are a sofa/some armchairs …
It looks friendly/busy/modern.

Expressing opinions

I agree.
I completely agree with that.
I agree that …
I love fashion.
I love being outdoors.
I really like clothes.
To me, fashion's fun.
I think fashion's cool.
It sounds really interesting.
I don't really agree with that.
I disagree that …
Sorry, but I don't think that's a very good idea!
I'm not sure about that.
I don't think it's a good thing.
I can't stand this kind of mess.
I don't really care.

Discussing opinions

I think Katrina is best because she's older.

I don't think Katrina's suitable because she doesn't want to study Psychology.

Yes, but Martin speaks better English.

Personally, I think people care too much about fashion.

I can't live without my CD player.

I don't know much about fashion.

I don't agree because …

In my opinion …

The accommodation doesn't matter.

She's wearing too much make-up.

She's got too many tattoos.

His trousers are too baggy.

She isn't old enough to be a model.

Polite requests and responding

Polite requests

Can you enter your PIN, please?

Could you put it in the bag?

Can I try it on?

Could I have a bigger size?

Is it okay if I pay by card?

Responding

Sure, no problem.

Yes, of course.

I'm sorry but …

Going shopping

Can I help you?

We're just looking, thanks.

I like this one. What do you think?

What size are you looking for?

The fitting room is over there.

This one's too small.

Do you want to try this one/that?

Is that size better?

Future plans

Talking about future plans and careers

Which subjects are you going to choose?

I'm definitely going to do English.

What do you want to do?

I'm planning to have a gap year.

I want to travel.

What would you like to do in your gap year?

I'd like to go to Italy.

In my future career, I'd like to work with computers.

Are you going on holiday this summer?

We're flying to Florida. I can't wait!

Discussing customs

Discussing customs

Most people have cereal and milk.

Generally, people have lunch at home.

We don't usually eat takeaways.

Chicken is traditional/very popular.

Responding

Really?

Yes, it's the same in my country.

It's similar/different in my country because people work very late.

Making arrangements

Making arrangements

Would you like to come for lunch?

Are you free today?

Are you doing anything later today?

Are you going out this evening/at the weekend?

How about next Sunday instead?

Why don't we …?

Shall we …?

Accepting

That would be lovely, thanks.

That sounds great!

That's a good idea.

Refusing

I'm sorry, I can't. I'm going shopping with my mum.

I'm afraid I've got an appointment.

Speculating about the future

Young people will be able to travel more.

People will have to go home to visit relatives.

People will probably learn more about other cultures.

People will definitely work abroad more in the future.

There will be many more visitors to interesting cities.

Many historic places won't be special any more.

If the school bans mobile phones, pupils will concentrate better in lessons.

It might snow tomorrow.

Pollution from planes may increase global warming.

Describing holidays

Describing your holiday

Our holiday was terrible/boring/exciting!

We had a fantastic/horrible time!

First, we had a really bad/long/scary journey.

After that we lost our luggage/passports.

And then it rained/snowed every day.

In the end we came home early/changed hotels.

Showing interest

How was your holiday?

What happened?

Really?

Oh, no!

So what did you do?

You're joking!

Asking for and giving advice

Asking for advice

Can you recommend anything?

Where should we stay?

What should we see?

Do you think we should book?

What's the best way to do it?

Which is the best gallery/museum?

What about nightlife?

Giving advice

Go by train.

You must go to Montmartre.

You should definitely stay there.

I don't think you should take the coach.

Don't fly.

There's loads to do! You'll love it!

If you like modern art, I think you should go to the Pompidou Centre.

It's best to take a guided tour.

Describing sports

It's a very popular sport in Italy/all over the world.

People play in summer/in winter/all year round.

It's an indoor/outdoor game.

Each team has six players.

To play the game, you need a ball.

It's very exciting.

Giving instructions

First of all, you switch it on.

Then you select from the menu.

You have to charge the battery/it.

Just follow the instructions.

Don't forget to switch it off.

Making complaints

What the customer says

I'd like a refund, please.

It doesn't work properly.

I'm really not happy about this.

Could I speak to the manager, please?

What the shop assistant says

What exactly is the problem?

Have you got the receipt?

We can exchange it if you like.

I'm afraid we can't give refunds.

I'm sorry, there's nothing I can do.

Telephoning

Hi, Carrie speaking.

Hi, it's Zack.

Is Grace there?

She isn't here at the moment. Can I take a message?

Why don't you try her mobile?

Could I speak to Carrie, please?

Who's calling?

Just a minute, I'll get her.

Could you call me as soon as you can?

Speak to you soon.

answer key

self-assessment test 1

1 2 great-grandfather, 3 daughter-in-law, 4 uncle, 5 only, 6 niece

2 2 Brave, 3 do, 4 determined, 5 got, 6 designed

3 2 'm /am doing, 3 was waiting, 4 go, 5 doesn't eat, 6 isn't/is not writing, 7 didn't see, 8 met, 9 were studying

4 2 Who are you phoning? 3 What was Fiona doing when I called? 4 How many brothers and sisters have you got? 5 What time did Ron get up yesterday? 6 When is your boyfriend's birthday? 7 Where did you have lunch on Saturday?

5 2 'm/am going, 3 got, 4 were having, 5 rent, 6 fell, 7 're/are making

6 1 b, 2 e, 3 g, 4 a, 5 f, 6 c, 7 d

7 1 ✗, 2 ✗, 3 ✓, 4 ✗, 5 ✗, 6 ✓

8 1 g, 2 d, 3 c, 4 a, 5 f, 6 h, 7 e, 8 b

self-assessment test 2

1 2 tight, 3 afford, 4 temporary, 5 part-time, 6 mean

2 2 lend, 3 take, 4 experience, 5 interview, 6 bargain, 7 generous, 8 long

3 2 to begin, 3 waiting, 4 to swim, 5 eating, 6 going, 7 to learn

4 2 to work, 3 Do, 4 the worst, 5 going, 6 not old enough, 7 to study

5 2 better, 3 the messiest, 4 too baggy, 5 shorter than, 6 the most comfortable, 7 as rewarding as

6 1 C, 2 B, 3 C, 4 A, 5 B, 6 A, 7 B

7 2 on; e, 3 help; b, 4 pay; c, 5 too; a

8 2 much, 3 To, 4 agree, 5 looks, 6 care

self-assessment test 3

1 2 sausages, 3 strict, 4 loaf, 5 had, 6 grapes, 7 cheese

2 2 juice, 3 get, 4 put, 5 make, 6 contain, 7 do, 8 piece

3 2 don't have to, 3 were, 4 should, 5 aren't allowed to, 6 can

4 2 could punish, 3 should lose, 4 can't vote, 5 must stop, 6 didn't have to do, 7 had to join, 8 shouldn't eat

5 2 Ø, 3 Ø, 4 a, 5 The, 6 a, 7 the, 8 a, 9 the, 10 Ø, 11 an

6 1 ✓ 2 ✓ 3 ✓ 4 ✗ 5 ✗ 6 ✗ 7 ✓ 8 ✓

7 2 That would be 3 don't you bring 4 great idea 5 Shall we 6 you free 7 afraid 8 can't

8 2 Really? 3 different 4 Personally 5 sure 6 agree

self-assessment test 4

1 2 c, 3 g, 4 a, 5 h, 6 d, 7 e, 8 b

2 2 c, 3 a, 4 c, 5 b, 6 a, 7 b

3 2 Have you ever got sunburnt? 3 We've/have just collected the luggage. 4 Robert's/has never scored twenty points in one match. 5 I've/have already competed in four tournaments. 6 Have they gone through passport control yet?

4 2 'll/will come, 3 'm/am not doing, 4 'll/will be able to, 5 are getting, 6 might/may rain, 7 won't eat, 8 might/may not pass

5 2 ran, 3 will definitely travel, 4 driven, 5 have to, 6 already

6 1 ✓, 2 ✗, 3 ✗, 4 ✗, 5 ✓, 6 ✗

7 1 b, 2 b, 3 c, 4 a, 5 c, 6 a

8 2 way, Don't, 3 recommend, must, 4 How, terrible, 5 should, definitely

self-assessment test 5

1 2 off, 3 floods, 4 plug, 5 sea, 6 press

2 2 set, 3 extinct, 4 gadget, 5 uninhabited, 6 eruption

3 2 A desert, where, 3 A remote control, which/that, 4 A jungle, where, 5 A customer, who/that, 6 An answering machine, which/that

4 2 They've/have been at school since eight o'clock. 3 I haven't/have not talked to Martha for a long time. 4 How long have you known him? 5 We haven't/have not seen our teacher since Christmas. 6 Lee's/has lived in France for five years.

5 2 arrives, 3 won't be able to, 4 is, 5 come, 6 doesn't come

6 2 It used to snow a lot in this part of the country. 3 The temperature here yesterday was very high. 4 When the children heard an explosion, they screamed with fear. 5 Did your father use to play football when he was a teenager? 6 We didn't use to fly but now we go by plane everywhere

7 1 b, 2 c, 3 f, 4 a, 5 c, 6 a

8 2 work properly, 3 refund, 4 receipt, 5 keep it, 6 exchange it, 7 speak to, 8 problem, 9 I'd like, 10 there's nothing

9 1 First, 2 Then, 3 have, 4 Just, 5 don't

self-assessment test 6

1 2 d, 3 b, 4 g, 5 a, 6 h, 7 e, 8 c

2 2 disappointing, 3 surprised, 4 embarrassing, 5 interesting, 6 terrified, 7 pleased

3 2 threatened, 3 wouldn't/would not drop; were, 4 wore; wouldn't/would not get, 5 'd/would look; didn't/did not use

4 2 are committed, 3 has been translated, 4 was attacked, 5 have been blamed, 6 are downloaded, 7 were protected

5 2 I asked my older brother to help me with my Maths homework. 3 My father advised my mother to go to the doctor. 4 Our teacher ordered Eddie and Nick to stop playing football in the classroom. 5 My older sister told me not to take her clothes.

6 1 c 2 c 3 b 4 b 5 a

7 1 Sam 2 Ellie 3 Michael 4 Michael 5 Ellie 6 Sam

8 1 e 2, b 3, a 4, d 5
    2 d 2, c 3, f 4, a 5, e 6

exam test 1

1 1 ✓, 2 ✗, 3 ✗, 4 ✓, 5 ✗, 6 ✗

2 1 September, 2 Hawkshead, 3 11 a.m., 4 comfortable, 5 £20, 6 contact

3 2 a, 3 c, 4 b, 5 c, 6 a, 7 b, 8 c, 9 c, 10 b

4 2 passed, 3 for, 4 forms, 5 because, 6 long, 7 was, 8 When, 9 afford, 10 going

exam test 2

1 1 E, 2 D, 3 C, 4 A

2 1 b, 2 c, 3 a, 4 a, 5 a, 6 b

3 2 freedom, 3 arguments, 4 responsibilities, 5 washing, 6 invitation, 7 amazing, 8 cycling, 9 active, 10 unhealthy, 11 exciting

4 1 I have never travelled outside Europe. 2 Can I have a large glass of orange juice? 3 David enjoys hanging out with friends in the evening. 4 Has she ever won a prize in a competition? 5 Where do you usually go on holiday in the summer? 6 We will definitely finish this project next week. 7 A car is more expensive than a bike. 8 Lucy and I might go sightseeing in the afternoon. 9 My friend phoned while I was doing my homework./ I was doing my homework when my friend phoned? 10 Their children are not allowed to watch TV after 8 p.m.

exam test 3

1 1 c, 2 b, 3 d, 4 c, 5 b, 6 d

2 1 ✓, 2 ✓, 3 ✗, 4 ✗, 5 ✓, 6 ✗

3 2 Tom to eat, 3 was asked by, 4 as fast as, 5 hasn't (has not) rained, 6 Mary to move, 7 studied hard, 8 has been opened, 9 disappointed by, 10 not to make

4 2 If/When, 3 where, 4 his, 5 which/ that, 6 than, 7 to, 8 was, 9 were, 10 a